John Kenneth Galbraith was American Ambassador to India from 1961–3, and for many years, Paul M. Warburg Professor of Economics at Harvard University. He was born in 1908 in Ontario, Canada. After graduating in agriculture at Toronto and taking a Ph.D. at the University of California, he became Social Science Research Council Fellow at Cambridge, England, and went on to teach at the universities of California, Princeton and Harvard (1945–75). In 1970–71 he spent two terms at Cambridge University as Fellow at Trinity College and Visiting Lecturer at the faculty of Economics and Politics.

During the war, at the American Office of Price Administration, he headed the wartime price-control activities, and later was a director of the U.S. Strategic Bombing Survey and of the Office of Security Policy, receiving the Medal of Freedom and the President's Certificate of Merit for his work. He has been closely identified with the Democratic Party.

Professor Galbraith has contributed to leading American journals and reviews. His books include *A Theory of Price Control*, *American Capitalism*, *The Affluent Society* (which held its place on the best-seller lists for some thirty weeks), *The Great Crash 1929*, *The Liberal Hour*, *The Non-potable Scotch* and *The New Industrial State*. He is also the author of a book of satirical sketches, *The McLandress Dimension*; a best-selling novel, *The Triumph*; a study of Indian painting, *Indian Painting: Scene, Themes and Legends* (with M. S. Randhawa), *Ambassador's Journal*, *Economics, Peace and Laughter*, *A Chinese Passage*, a record of his visit to China, *Economics and the Public Purpose*, *Money: Whence It Came, Where It Went*, *The Age of Uncertainty*, *Almost Everyone's Guide to Economics*, *The Nature of Mass Poverty*, *The Anatomy of Power* and a volume of memoirs, *A Life in Our Times*. He delivered the Reith lectures in 1966.

The author, who is an enthusiastic skier, is married and has three sons. Much of his writing is done in Switzerland and on an old farm in Vermont.

# THE GREAT CRASH
# 1929

*John Kenneth Galbraith*

**PENGUIN BOOKS**
*in association with Hamish Hamilton*

PENGUIN BOOKS

Published by the Penguin Group
27 Wrights Lane, London w8 5TZ, England
Viking Penguin Inc., 40 West 23rd Street, New York, New York 10010, USA
Penguin Books Australia Ltd, Ringwood, Victoria, Australia
Penguin Books Canada Ltd, 2801 John Street, Markham, Ontario, Canada L3R 1B4
Penguin Books (NZ) Ltd, 182–190 Wairau Road, Auckland 10, New Zealand

Penguin Books Ltd, Registered Offices: Harmondsworth, Middlesex, England

First published in the USA 1954
Published in Great Britain by Hamish Hamilton 1955
Published in Pelican Books 1961
Reprinted 1963, 1966, 1968, 1969, 1971
Reprinted with revisions 1975
Reprinted 1977, 1980, 1984, 1987, 1988

Printed and bound in Great Britain by
Cox & Wyman Ltd, Reading
Set in Monotype Imprint

TO
CATHERINE ATWATER
GALBRAITH

# CONTENTS

# FOREWORD TO THE 1975 EDITION

THE pages that follow tell of the greatest cycle of speculative boom and collapse in modern times – since, in fact, the South Sea Bubble. There is merit in keeping alive the memory of those days. For it is neither public regulation nor the improving moral tone of corporate promoters, brokers, customer's men, market operators, bankers, and mutual fund managers which prevents these recurrent outbreaks and their aftermath. It is the recollection of how, on some past occasion, illusion replaced reality and people got rimmed.

In the wake of the 1929 crash, and with a view to preventing another runaway boom and the associated abuse, the Congress passed some tolerably astringent legislation including the Securities Exchange Act of 1934. It was not, at the time, especially necessary. Markets and financial adventure were then and for a long while after restrained not by S.E.C. but by the memory of what happened to so many in 1929.

By the sixties this memory had dimmed. Almost everything described in this book had reappeared, sometimes in only a slightly different guise. Instead of the investment trusts there were now the mutual funds. Matching Blue Ridge and Shenandoah in general scope and financial peril were the International Investment Trust and the Fund of Funds. Matching and possibly surpassing the vaulting imagination of Harrison Williams and Waddill Catchings, of Central States Electric and Goldman, Sachs was that of Edward Cowett and Bernard Cornfeld, the miracle men of I.O.S. The admiration for skill in deployment of corporate capital that was once lavished on Samuel Insull and Howard Hopson settled now on the men who were parlaying smaller firms into big conglomerates. There were glamour stocks in both periods; in both periods glamour was a substitute for substance. Scholars and politicians lent their names and blessings to the new promotions as had their counterparts forty years before. In the sixties as in the twenties men intended by nature for mentally undemanding toil became rich for a little while. It was only that the market was going up. Some things in 1970 were worse. Wall Street houses in the sixties were markedly more incompetent in their management than in the twenties and expanded much more recklessly. The consequences when the collapse came were far more troublesome than in 1929.

The new laws were not without effect. The gamiest of the promotions of the sixties had to be sold to foreigners – thus the offshore funds. There was much less speculation on margin. In both periods leverage – the purchase of common stocks with bonds or debentures allowing the investor to have all of the increase in value with minimal personal outlay – was redis-covered and heralded as the financial innovation of the age. But the suppression of the holding company kept leverage from being used as extravagantly in the sixties as in the twenties. In consequence it went less violently into reverse – as leverage does when a firm must pay interest out of declining earnings from common stock. The collapse of the Van Sweringen rail-roads in the thirties was the result of reverse leverage. Penn Central went down only as the result of gross mismanagement. The day of reckoning in 1970 was disagreeable – and the mag-nitude of the market decline was not so different from that in the autumn months of 1929. But it did not become cumulative. And the effect on consumer spending, business investment and the economy generally was far less severe.

Yet the lesson is evident. The story of the boom and crash of 1929 is worth telling for its own sake. Great drama joined in those months with a luminous insanity. But there is the more sombre purpose. As a protection against financial illusion or insanity, memory is far better than law. When the memory of the 1929 disaster failed, law and regulation no longer sufficed. For protecting people from the cupidity of others and their own, history is highly utilitarian. It sustains memory and memory serves the same purpose as the S.E.C. and, on the record, is far more effective.

The main body of the text of this edition is identical with that of its predecessor. I've retained in slightly abbreviated form, in the pages following, the introduction to the second edition for it tells of the origins of this book and of the exceedingly lively reception that it was accorded by the Senate Banking and Currency Committee and Senator Homer Capehart of Indiana. And there are a few changes in the final chapter – which, however, still speculates on the effect on the economy of the next really great crash. All else is as before.

JOHN KENNETH GALBRAITH

# ON THE ORIGINS OF THIS BOOK

I WROTE this book during the summer and autumn of 1954. At the time I was engaged on the manuscript which eventually became *The Affluent Society*. Or, more precisely, after months of ineffective and frustrating labour which had produced a set of chapters so vapid in content and repulsive in style that I could not bear to read them, I was totally stalled. Suicide seemed the only answer; unfortunately it was an exceptionally lovely summer in southern Vermont. My neighbour, Arthur M. Schlesinger, Jr, had once made the modest request that I do the definitive work on the Great Depression. It would be convenient, he thought, for his work on Roosevelt. I resolved to compromise and write a book on the dramatic days that ushered the depression in.

I never enjoyed writing a book more; indeed, it is the only one I remember in no sense as a labour but as a joy. I did the research in the Baker Library at Dartmouth College, working under the Orosco murals on the ground floor. They somehow supported the mood of unreality, gargantuan excess and hovering disaster of the months before the crash. And, as might happen toward the end of the morning or the end of the afternoon if this mood became too overpowering, one could walk out into the sunshine, across the most exquisite village common in all New England, and have a martini and a good meal at the Hanover Inn. I scamped my teaching that autumn to work on the manuscript; when I left it with the publisher, I felt that I was saying goodbye to a close and valued companion.

2

My labours during the autumn had been made to seem rather
more relevant by the contemporary boom in the stock market.
This was small compared with 1929; it was very small compared with the bidding up of values and the bidding down of
yields that subsequently took place. But it was plain that an
increasing number of persons were coming to the conclusion –
the conclusion that is the common denominator of all speculative episodes – that they were predestined by luck, an
unbeatable system, divine favour, access to inside information,
or exceptional financial acumen to become rich without work.

In the spring the boom, or boomlet, continued. The Democrats had won the Congressional elections the previous autumn;
the Republicans had the White House for the first time since
Hoover. It seemed worth the while of the Senate Committee
on Banking and Currency to see if the boom portended another
bust. Chairman William Fulbright decided that it would be a
quiet and friendly investigation. I was called to testify. This
was not entirely by accident. While testifying a few weeks
earlier on another matter before another Committee, I used
the opportunity to tell Mr Robert A. Wallace and Mr Myer
Feldman, two of the distinguished and self-effacing men who
serve the public by serving Congressmen and their Committees
and then staff members of the Banking and Currency Committee, of what I had under way. An invitation to testify on
the 1929 experience came promptly and was not an unbearable
surprise.

I believe that almost everyone enjoys testifying before a
friendly Congressional Committee or even a moderately cen-
sorious one. For the moment you are an oracle, a minor oracle
to be sure, but possessed of knowledge important for the future
of the Republic. Your words go down in an imperishable, if

sadly unread, record. Newspapermen, one or two at least, are present to transmit your better thoughts to the world or, more frequently, your worst ones, for these, being improbable, have novelty and seem more likely to merit a minor headline. An audience is on hand. Except for an exceedingly dramatic investigation, this audience is always about the same. Apart from watchdogs from the Executive Departments and one's friends, it consists of connoisseurs of the Congressional Hearings who attend them every day. Quite a few are of advanced years and none has alternative employment, and if they are not our best, they must at least be our most widely informed citizenry. Labour rackets, the missile gap, influence on the FCC, the economic outlook, the organization of the National Security Council are all grist for their highly diversified mill. They listen attentively and critically; and Congressional Hearing has about it a touch of theatre and this is helped by having a competent and critical house.

The witness at the Congressional Hearing is treated with courtesy and deference, which in politics is always a trifle more effusive and therefore a great deal more pleasant than in any other walk of life. He must, however, expect to be seduced into statements damaging to his case if that is beneficial to the political needs or beliefs of an interrogator. This adds interest, and the stakes are not very high. My professional colleagues occasionally complain of the time they spend in preparing for or attending these inquiries. This is strictly for the purpose of impressing the others at the Department meeting. They enjoy it and wouldn't dream of declining.

3

I testified at the morning session of the stock market hearings on Tuesday, 8 March 1955. Several witnesses from the financial world, including Mr G. Keith Funston and a bevy of vice-commissars of the New York Stock Exchange, had preceded me. The market had reacted to their testimony with admirable equanimity perhaps because they had said nothing although they had said it very well. Nor was my testimony sensational. I had brought along the proofs of this book; I drew on them to tell what had happened twenty-five years before, in 1928 and 1929. Toward the end I suggested that history *could* repeat itself, although I successfully resisted all invitations to predict when. I did urge a stiff tightening of margin requirements as a precautionary step. Similar action to minimize the use of credit for speculation had been taken during the war when the speculative enthusiasm was much less. Through it all the newspapermen sat gazing with partly open mouths at the ceiling of the Senate caucus chamber or looking down briefly to scribble a random note. An aide appeared occasionally, sidling along the wall behind the Committee, to pass a note to one of the Senators. The audience, I knew from waiting my turn on earlier occasions, was following me closely and, on occasion, exchanging a critical aside on my facts, logic, or diction. As the testimony gave way to questions, more Senators came in. This is perhaps the most trying time of any hearing. Each in his turn apologizes graciously for being late and then asks the question that has occurred to him on the way over. The question is always the same; and the Senator does not know that it has been asked before:

SENATOR ROBERTSON: Well, Professor, we have been told by all the witnesses so far that present stock prices are not too high? What is your view on that?

SENATOR IVES: You do not think we are faced with a bust, do you?

SENATOR MONRONEY: I am wondering if there is any substance to the oft-repeated reason for the new high levels ... That the stock market is merely catching up with the inflationary boom. . .

SENATOR PAYNE: I am sorry I came in late ... would you want to indicate whether or not some of these increases have perhaps more truly reflected the true value of stocks in relation to their earnings?

The experienced witness observes that the question, though it bears a resemblance to some already asked, has been formulated in a novel way. Then he gives an answer which is the same in substance but decently different in form from those offered before. The audience is especially appreciative of able handling of such details.

Toward the end of the morning, interest appeared to increase. First one and then several photographers appeared. Then a newsreel camera or two. Through the weariness that develops with even so modest a sojourn in the public eye, I thought I sensed a certain tension. I remember noticing that the normal attrition of the Committee – which on a subject such as economics can leave one in a matter of an hour or so with only the Chairman and a precautionary member of the opposition – was not taking place. All Senators were staying. And soon I was the only one in the room who did not know the reason. The stock market was taking a nasty plunge.

I still did not know the reason when the hearing recessed at 12.57, just as a harried man from CBS came dashing into the chamber followed by two beasts of burden carrying a vast poundage of electronic marvels. He had been off in another room photographing Dulles. The real history had passed him by. In response to his almost tearful plea, I repeated several minutes of my testimony to an open window. The substitution of this for the Senators led to a considerable release from inhibition. I rather let myself go with the gestures – at times grave and statesmanlike, at others perhaps a trifle flamboyant. It was this that the world and my children saw.

I still did not realize what had happened until someone handed me a paper with a big headline. The *New York Times* industrials went off 7 points on the day. Stocks lost $3 billion in value on the New York Stock Exchange.

## 4

Back in Cambridge the next few days were among the most interesting in my memory. The phone rang continuously – so continuously that my secretary went home in annoyance, leaving me to answer it myself. Some of the calls were from the very great Ed Murrow, who wanted me to extend my remarks for an even larger audience. I declined. A few wanted to know if I was likely to say anything that would affect the market in the near future. I promised them silence. The rest merely wished to denounce me for destroying their dream.

The telephone calls were supplemented, beginning the morning after the testimony, by a mountain of mail. All was unfavourable. Some was denunciatory; more was belligerent; much was prayerful. The belligerent threatened various forms of physical violence. My wife professed particular concern over five communications from a man in Florida announcing that he was on his way north to kill me. Her alarm subsided when I pointed out (having thoughtfully checked the point myself) that all were postmarked Palm Beach. The prayerful all said they were beseeching their God to have me meet with a bad accident – some were asking that I be deprived of life, some of limb, and the minimum request was that I lose all ability to open my mouth. On Wednesday night, I crawled into bed reflecting, with less than characteristic piety, on all of the prayers that were spiralling up at that moment petitioning my dismemberment or destruction. I thought of saying a word on my own behalf and then struggled with the shattering thought that these matters might be decided by majority vote.

The next morning dawned bright and clear, and my wife and I decided to take a day away from it all. We went to Mount Snow, Vermont, to ski. Toward the end of the afternoon I turned from shaded and hard snow to some that had been softened by the sun and had a bad spill and broke my leg. The papers carried a note about my mishap. I now heard from those whose belief in the existence of a just and omnipotent God had been deeply strengthened.

A few days later, the market started up again. My mail fell off and stopped. A representative collection of the letters was posted in a seminar room and viewed admiringly by students for weeks. But there was more to come.

## 5

The state of Indiana was then represented in the Senate of the United States by Homer E. Capehart. He was a Republican, conservative and wealthy. It is possible, as partisan Democrats, at least, believed, that the people of Indiana could have had a better representative. But he was not a wicked man. His colleagues found him pleasant. So had I on previous brief encounter. These were the diminuendo days of Senator Joseph McCarthy. Unlike his colleague, William Jenner, Capehart had never been much involved in McCarthy's crusades. The senior Republican on the Banking and Currency Committee, he had not been present on the day I testified.

On 20 March, in the course of a network television programme, Senator Capehart announced that I would be recalled before the Committee to answer for having spoken favourably of communism and then, presumably, having advanced its cause by collapsing the market. I had had some warning. A gentleman from the Senator's office had called me a day or two before to see if I admitted to authorship of the offending encomium. The programme had been filmed the day before. Also present on the programme was a good and gallant friend, Senator A. S. Mike Monroney of Oklahoma. After extemporizing a brilliant defence of my dereliction, he called me to tell me what was coming.

The praise of communism had been extracted from a pamphlet of the National Planning Association dealing with problems of postwar Europe. It noted that the communists had a better reputation for sincerity and determination in attacking old social grievances and that they also had a solution to the problem of petty nationalism by asserting the higher loyalty to the worker's state. But Senator Capehart's case was not without flaw. The kind words were marred by a caveat, expressing suspicion and distaste of communism on other grounds, which had been put into the very middle of the paragraph for the precise purpose of preventing any inconvenient use, a precaution normal in those days. The Senator had thought it necessary to delete this offending clause, a distinctly noticeable act. The pamphlet had been based on a lecture given originally at the University of Notre Dame in, of all states, Indiana. An earlier version had been published by the University. The pamphlet had been endorsed in principle by Allen Dulles, the brother of the Secretary of State, and Milton Eisenhower, the brother of the President, an underwriting which, however, could cause some doubts as to the utter originality of the ideas advanced. Even a brilliant improviser like Joe McCarthy might have wished for a better case.

A day or so later, the Senator made the further discovery that, at a meeting of the American Economic Association not long before, a conservative professional colleague had jeopardized any possible reputation for understatement by saying that I was, though perhaps unconsciously, 'one of the most effective enemies of capitalism and democracy' in all the land. But this evidence did not retrieve matters as much as might have been hoped. My friend thought me dangerous because I was too soft on industrial monopoly.

Like most other liberal academicians, I had been a thoughtful observer of the methods of the Wisconsin Titus Oates. Two had always seemed to me worth adopting by anyone attacked. The first was to avoid defence of one's self and instead assault the accuser. The second was to avoid any suspicion, however remote, of personal modesty. I put these methods to test when I heard of the charges. I sent a telegram to the network carrying the programme, to key stations, the wire services, and to important papers indicting the Senator for incompetence. I identified incompetence with failure to know my views and these I implied – indeed, I stated – were an imperishable chapter in the intellectual history of our time. I followed the wire a few days later with a press conference, which, by a fortunate accident of travel, I was able to hold in Indiana.

The effect of my efforts, I am persuaded, was to convert an attack that otherwise would have been wholly ignored into front-page news. Neither of us was ever so featured before and I trust will never be so featured again. But I have no complaint about the press. It concluded that I had been assailed for being unkind to the stock market. This it refused to condemn as seriously subversive.

The Senator then took the floor of the Senate for a further denunciation. Some of this centred on my characterization of communism as a monolithic force, which he regarded as seriously suspect. 'Mr President, "monolithic" means like a monument, or a pillar of strength. . . That is like describing communism as a monument or as a pillar of strength; or, as we used to say, like the Rock of Gibraltar.'

But by now he was losing power. He said, handsomely, that

there were things in the offending pamphlet with which 'we can all agree'. It was unfair, he added, to suggest that he had called me a Red. After some further bickering in the Committee, he subsided. The Senator has had no further reputation as a witch-hunter. I like to think that he himself was plucked as a brand from the burning. I filed a further and rather sanctimonious statement with the Committee but was not recalled.

## 6

On 21 April 1955, the book was finally published. The publisher had some months before decided that the volume needed a good strong jacket. This turned out to be a bright and very visible red. With this colour and all the excitement of the preceding weeks, it seemed certain that the interest in the book would be overwhelming. In the end the response was admirable but the early market was very orderly. Indeed, depressingly so. One evening I was coming through the old La Guardia terminal on my way to Boston and I paused as usual to eye the window of the little bookshop on the way to the ramp. As usual there was no sign of the bright red jacket.

The lady asked me if I wanted something and I summoned all of my resources of courage and verisimilitude and said, 'I seem to remember a lot of recent discussion about a book – I forget the name of the author, maybe Galbraith – but I think it was called *The Great Crash*.'

She replied, 'That's certainly not a title you could sell in an airport.'

# A NOTE ON SOURCES

*In recent times numerous authors and publishers have come to suppose that readers are offended by footnotes. I have no desire to offend or even in the slightest way to discourage any solvent customer, but I regard this supposition as silly. No literate person can possibly be disturbed by a little small type at the bottom of a page, and everyone, professional and lay reader alike, needs to know on occasion the credentials of a fact. Footnotes also provide an exceedingly good index of the care with which a subject has been researched.*

*However, there is also a line between adequacy and pedantry. In this book where I have drawn on public documents, books, magazine articles, or special sources of any kind I have indicated the source. However, much of the story of 1929 is to be found in the general and financial press of the time. Systematic citation of these sources would involve endless references to the same papers. This I have not done. It means in general that if no source is given, the reader can assume it was in the* New York Times, *the* Wall Street Journal, *and the other papers of general circulation of the day.*

# CHAPTER I

# A YEAR TO REMEMBER

## I

SOME years, like some poets and politicians and some lovely women, are singled out for fame far beyond the common lot, and 1929 was clearly such a year. Like 1066, 1776, and 1914, it is a year that everyone remembers. One went to college before 1929, was married after 1929, or wasn't even born in 1929, which bespeaks total innocence. A reference to 1929 has become shorthand for the events of that autumn. For a decade, whenever Americans have been afflicted with doubt as to the durability of their current state of prosperity, they have asked 'Will it be 1929 all over again?' And even after a quarter of a century, this is still a year with a singular political personality. Just as Republican orators for a generation after Appomattox made use of the bloody shirt, so for a generation Democrats have been warning that to elect Republicans is to invite another disaster like that of 1929. The defeat of the Democratic candidate in 1952 was widely attributed to the unfortunate appearance at the polls of too many youths who knew only by hearsay of the horrors of those days.

It would be good to know whether, indeed, we shall some day have another 1929. However, the much less pretentious task of this book – the only task which social science in its present state allows – is to tell what happened in 1929 and immediately before and thereafter. Much of the story concerns the stock market, and in part it represents an effort to put right an error that has long been fashionable among economic historians. The stock market crash in the autumn of 1929 has long been held to have been a somewhat secondary event.

25

Beneath its froth more serious forces were at work. These, well prior to the market collapse and quite apart from anything that happened in Wall Street, were shaping things up for a serious depression. This explanation was attractive in downtown New York, for it at least partially absolved the stock market from the formidable responsibility of the depression. In my view, this puts the wrong face on matters. There is an essential unity in economic phenomena; no Chinese wall separates the fiduciary from the real. Wall Street – as its prophets for other purposes concede – is of considerable importance in the American economy. The stock market crash and the speculation which made it inevitable had an important effect on the performance, or rather the malperformance, of the economy in the ensuing months and years.

2

As a year, 1929 has always been peculiarly the property of the economists. It was a year of notable economic events; indeed, in that year began the most momentous economic occurrence in the history of the United States, the ordeal of the Great Depression. In many ways this preoccupation with economics is unfortunate, for 1929 was a year of many marvels. In particular, it was one of those years that marvellously illuminate human motives and the very wellsprings of human behaviour. Historians and novelists always have known that tragedy wonderfully reveals the nature of man. But, while they have made rich use of war, revolution, and poverty, they have been singularly neglectful of financial panics. And one can relish the varied idiocy of human action during a panic to the full, for, while it is a time of great tragedy, nothing is being lost but money.

In the autumn of 1929 the mightiest of Americans were, for a brief time, revealed as human beings. Like most humans, most of the time, they did some very foolish things. On the whole, the greater the earlier reputation for omniscience, the more serene the previous idiocy, the greater the foolishness now exposed. Things that in other times were concealed by a heavy facade of dignity now stood exposed, for the panic suddenly, almost obscenely, snatched this façade away. We are seldom vouchsafed a glance behind this barrier; in our society the counterpart of the Kremlin walls is the thickly stuffed shirt. The social historian must always be alert to his opportunities, and there have been few like 1929.

## 3

The years following the stock market crash produced a notable outpouring of books, articles, congressional documents, and reports, all exposing Wall Street for what it was. A certain amount of dubious behaviour was brought to light and Wall Street was well pilloried for its crimes.

It will perhaps already be evident that this book has no similar motive. I have never adhered to the view that Wall Street is uniquely evil, just as I have never found it possible to accept with complete confidence the alternative view, rather more palatable in sound financial circles, that it is uniquely wise.

Moreover, implicit in this hue and cry was the notion that somewhere on Wall Street – possibly at Number 23 and possibly on an obscure corridor in one of the high buildings – there was a *deus ex machina* who somehow engineered the boom and bust. This notion that great misadventures are the work of great and devious adventurers, and that the latter can and must be found if we are to be safe, is a popular one in our time. Since the search for the architect of the Wall Street debacle, we have had a hue and cry for the man who let the Russians into Western Europe, the man who lost China, and the man who thwarted MacArthur in Korea. While this may be a harmless avocation, it does not suggest an especially good view of historical processes. No one was responsible for the great Wall Street crash. No one engineered the speculation that preceded it. Both were the product of the free choice and decisions of thousands of individuals. The latter were not led to the slaughter. They were impelled to it by the seminal lunacy which has always seized people who are seized in turn with the notion that they can become very rich. There were many Wall Streeters who helped to foster this insanity, and some of them will appear among the heroes of these pages. There was none who caused it.

4

To see the events of 1929 in the foregoing light is of some practical value. It has long been my feeling that the lessons of economics that reside in economic history are important and that history provides an interesting and even fascinating window on economic knowledge. For this reason this book is, perhaps, a bit more than a chronicle. There are frequent pauses to see how things work and why.

Finally, a good knowledge of what happened in 1929 remains our best safeguard against the recurrence of the more unhappy events of those days. Since 1929 we have enacted numerous laws designed to make securities speculation more honest and, it is hoped, more readily restrained. None of these is a perfect safeguard. The signal feature of the mass escape from reality that occurred in 1929 and before – and which has characterized every previous speculative outburst from the South Sea Bubble to the Florida land boom – was that it carried Authority with it. Governments were either bemused as were the speculators or they deemed it unwise to be sane at a time when sanity exposed one to ridicule, condemnation for spoiling the game, or the threat of severe political retribution.

In our own day, we can devoutly wish that we may be spared

the technically superlative disasters we have prepared for our-
selves in order to enjoy the minor vicissitudes of the business
cycle – of prosperity and depression and inflation and deflation.
If we are so favoured, we can count on some future period of
prosperity carrying us on into a mood of exhilarant optimism
and wild speculative frenzy. Instead of radio and investment
trusts, uranium mines or perhaps portable reactors will be the
new favourites. Or the speculative fever may strike land, oil, or
even Boston.

The wonder, indeed, is that since 1929 we have been spared
so long. One reason, without doubt, is that the experience of
1929 burned itself so deeply into the national consciousness. It
is worth hoping that a history such as this will keep bright that
immunizing memory for a little longer.

# CHAPTER II

# 'VISION AND BOUNDLESS HOPE AND OPTIMISM'

I

ON 4 December 1928 President Coolidge sent his last message on the state of the Union to the reconvening Congress. Even the most melancholy congressman must have found reassurance in his words. 'No Congress of the United States ever assembled, on surveying the state of the Union, has met with a more pleasing prospect than that which appears at the present time. In the domestic field there is tranquility and contentment ... and the highest record of years of prosperity. In the foreign field there is peace, the goodwill which comes from mutual understanding ...' He told the legislators that they and the country might 'regard the present with satisfaction and antici-pate the future with optimism'. And breaking sharply with the most ancient of our political conventions, he omitted to attri-bute this well-being to the excellence of the administration which he headed. 'The main source of these unexampled blessings lies in the integrity and character of the American people.'

A whole generation of historians has assailed Coolidge for the superficial optimism which kept him from seeing that a great storm was brewing at home and also more distantly abroad. This is grossly unfair. It requires neither courage nor prescience to predict disaster. Courage is required of the man who, when things are good, says so. Historians rejoice in crucifying the false prophet of the millennium. They never dwell on the mistake of the man who wrongly predicted Armageddon.

There was much that was good about the world of which Coolidge spoke. True, as liberal misanthropes have insisted, the rich were getting richer much faster than the poor were getting less poor. The farmers were unhappy and had been ever since the depression of 1920–1 had cut farm prices sharply but left costs high. Black people in the South and white people in the southern Appalachians continued to dwell in hopeless poverty. Fine old-English houses with high gables, leaded glass, and well-simulated half-timbering were rising in the country club district, while farther in town one encountered the most noisome slums outside the Orient.

All this notwithstanding, the twenties in America were a very good time. Production and employment were high and rising. Wages were not going up much, but prices were stable. Although many people were still very poor, more people were comfortably well-off, well-to-do, or rich than ever before. Finally, American capitalism was undoubtedly in a lively phase. Between 1925 and 1929, the number of manufacturing establishments increased from 183,900 to 206,700; the value of their output rose from $60·0 billions to $68·0 billions.[1] The Federal Reserve index of industrial production which had averaged only 67 in 1921 (1923–5 = 100) had risen to 110 by July 1928, and it reached 126 in June 1929.[2] In 1926, 4,301,000 automobiles were produced. Three years later, in 1929, production had increased by over a million to 5,358,000,[3] a figure which compares very decently with the 5,700,000 new car registrations of the opulent year of 1953. Business earnings were rising rapidly, and it was a good time to be in business. Indeed, even the most jaundiced histories of the era conceded,

1. U.S. Department of Commerce, Bureau of the Census, *Statistical Abstract of the United States, 1944–45.*

2. *Federal Reserve Bulletin,* December 1929.

3. Thomas Wilson, *Fluctuations in Income and Employment,* 3rd ed. New York (Pitman), 1948, p. 141.

tacitly, that times were good, for they nearly all join in taxing Coolidge for his failure to see that they were too good to last.

This notion of an iron law of compensation – the notion that the ten good years of the twenties had to be paid for by the ten bad ones of the thirties – is one to which it will be worthwhile to return.

2

One thing in the twenties should have been visible even to Coolidge. It concerned the American people of whose character he had spoken so well. Along with the sterling qualities he praised, they were also displaying an inordinate desire to get rich quickly with a minimum of physical effort. The first striking manifestation of this personality trait was in Florida. There, in the mid-twenties, Miami, Miami Beach, Coral Gables, the East Coast as far north as Palm Beach, and the cities over on the Gulf had been struck by the great Florida real estate boom. The Florida boom contained all of the elements of the classic speculative bubble. There was the indispensable element of substance. Florida had a better winter climate than New York, Chicago, or Minneapolis. Higher incomes and better transportation were making it increasingly accessible to the frost-bound North. The time indeed was coming when the annual flight to the South would be as regular and impressive as the migrations of the Canada Goose.

On that indispensable element of fact men and women had proceeded to build a world of speculative make-believe. This is a world inhabited not by people who have to be persuaded to believe but by people who want an excuse to believe. In the case of Florida, they wanted to believe that the whole peninsula would soon be populated by the holiday-makers and the sun-worshippers of a new and remarkably indolent era. So great would be the crush that beaches, bogs, swamps, and common scrubland would all have value. The Florida climate obviously did not ensure that this would happen. But it did enable people who wanted to believe it would happen so to believe.

However, speculation does not depend entirely on the capacity for self-delusion. In Florida land was divided into building lots and sold for a ten per cent down payment. Palpably, much of the unlovely terrain that thus changed hands was as repugnant to the people who bought it as to the passer-by. The buyers did not expect to live on it; it was not easy to suppose that anyone ever would. But these were academic considerations. The reality was that this dubious asset was gaining in value by the day and could be sold at a handsome profit in a fortnight. It is another feature of the speculative mood that, as time passes, the tendency to look beyond the simple fact of increasing values to the reasons on which it depends greatly diminishes. And there is no reason why anyone should do so as long as the supply of people who buy with the expectation of selling at a profit continues to be augmented at a sufficiently rapid rate to keep prices rising.

Through 1925 the pursuit of effortless riches brought people to Florida in satisfactorily increasing numbers. More land was subdivided each week. What was loosely called sea-shore became five, ten, or fifteen miles from the nearest brine. Suburbs became an astonishing distance from town. As the speculation spread northward, an enterprising Bostonian, Mr Charles Ponzi, developed a subdivision 'near Jacksonville'. It was approximately sixty-five miles west of the city. (In other respects Ponzi believed in good, compact neighbourhoods; he sold twenty-three lots to the acre.) In instances where the subdivision was close to town, as in the case of Manhattan Estates, which were 'not more than three-fourths of a mile from the prosperous and fast-growing city of Nettie', the city, as was so of Nettie, did not exist. The congestion of traffic into the state became so severe that in the autumn of 1925 the railroads were forced to proclaim an embargo on less essential freight, which included building materials for developing the subdivisions. Values rose wonderfully. Within forty miles of Miami 'inside' lots sold at from $8,000 to $20,000; waterfront lots brought from $15,000 to $25,000, and more or less bona fide sea-shore sites brought $20,000 to $75,000.[1]

However, in the spring of 1926, the supply of new buyers, so essential to the reality of increasing prices, began to fail. As 1928 and 1929 were to show, the momentum built up by a good boom is not dissipated in a moment. For a while in 1926 the increasing eloquence of the promoters offset the diminishing supply of prospects. (Even the cathedral voice of William Jennings Bryan, which once had thundered against the cross of gold, had been for a time enlisted in the sorry task of selling swampland.) But this boom was not left to collapse of its own weight. In the autumn of 1926, two hurricanes showed, in the words of Frederick Lewis Allen, 'what a Soothing Tropic Wind could do when it got a running start from the West Indies'.[2] The worst of these winds, on 18 September 1926, killed four hundred people, tore the roofs from thousands of houses, and piled tons of water and a number of elegant yachts into the streets of Miami. There was agreement that the storm had caused a healthy breathing spell in the boom, although its resumption was predicted daily. In the *Wall Street Journal* of 8 October 1926, one Peter O. Knight, an official of the Seaboard Air Line and a sincere believer in the future of Florida, acknowledged that some seventeen or eighteen thousand people were in need of assistance. But he added: 'The same Florida is

1. These details are principally from two articles on the Florida land boom by Homer B. Vandeblue in *The Journal of Land and Public Utility Economics*, May and August 1927.

2. *Only Yesterday*, New York (Harper), 1931, p. 280. Other details of the damage resulting from the hurricane are from this still fresh and lively book.

still there with its magnificent resources, its wonderful climate, and its geographical position. It is the Riviera of America.' He expressed concern that the solicitation of Red Cross funds for hurricane relief would 'do more damage permanently to Florida than would be offset by the funds received'.[1]

This reluctance to concede that the end has come is also in accordance with the classic pattern. The end had come in Florida. In 1925 bank clearings in Miami were $1,066,528,000; by 1928 they were down to $143,364,000.[2] Farmers who had sold their land at a handsome price and had condemned themselves as it later sold for double, treble, quadruple the original price, now on occasion got it back through a whole chain of subsequent defaults. Sometimes it was equipped with eloquently named streets and with sidewalks, street lamps, and taxes and assessments amounting to several times its current value.

The Florida boom was the first indication of the mood of the twenties and the conviction that God intended the American middle class to be rich. But that this mood survived the Florida collapse is still more remarkable. It was widely understood that things had gone to pieces in Florida. While the number of speculators was almost certainly small compared with the subsequent participation in the stock market, nearly every community contained a man who was known to have taken 'quite a beating' in Florida. For a century after the collapse of the South Sea Bubble, Englishmen regarded the most reputable joint stock companies with some suspicion. Even as the Florida boom collapsed, the faith of Americans in quick, effortless enrichment in the stock market was becoming every day more evident.

1. Vandeblue, op. cit., p. 114.
2. Allen, op. cit., p. 282.

3

It is hard to say when the stock market boom of the nineteen-twenties began. There were sound reasons why, during these years, the prices of common stocks should rise. Corporate earnings were good and growing. The prospect seemed benign. In the early twenties stock prices were low and yields favourable.

In the last six months of 1924, the prices of securities began to rise, and the increase was continued and extended through 1925. Thus at the end of May 1924, the *New York Times* average of the prices of twenty-five industrial stocks was 106; by the end of the year it was 134.[1] By 31 December 1925, it had gained very nearly another 50 points and stood at 181. The advance through 1925 was remarkably steady; there were only a couple of months when values did not show a net gain.

During 1926 there was something of a setback. Business was off a little in the early part of that year; it was thought by many that values the year before had risen unreasonably. February brought a sharp fall in the market, and March a rather abrupt collapse. The *Times* industrials went down from 181 at the

1. Throughout this book I have used the *New York Times* industrial averages as the shorthand designation of the level of security prices. This series is the arithmetical, unweighted average of the prices of twenty-five of what the *Times* describes as 'good, sound stocks with regular price changes and generally active markets'. The selection of the *Times* averages in preference to the Dow-Jones or other averages was largely arbitrary. The *Times* averages are the ones I have watched over the years; they are somewhat more accessible to the non-professional observer than the Dow-Jones averages. Also, while the latter are much better known, they carry in their wake a certain lore of market theory which is irrelevant for present purposes. The industrial rather than the railroad or combined average is cited because industrial stocks were the major focus of speculation and displayed the widest amplitude of movement. Unless there is indication to the contrary, values given are those at the close of the market for the date indicated.

beginning of the year to 172 at the end of February, and then dropped by nearly 30 points to 143 at the end of March. However, in April the market steadied and renewed its advance. Another mild setback occurred in October, just after the hurricane blew away the vestiges of the Florida boom, but again recovery was prompt. At the end of the year values were about where they had been at the beginning.

In 1927 the increase began in earnest. Day after day and month after month the price of stocks went up. The gains by later standards were not large, but they had an aspect of great reliability. Again in only two months in 1927 did the averages fail to show an increase. On 20 May, when Lindbergh took off from Roosevelt Field and headed for Paris, a fair number of citizens were unaware of the event. The market, which that day was registering another of its small but solid gains, had by then acquired a faithful band of devotees who spared no attention for more celestial matters.

In the summer of 1927 Henry Ford rang down the curtain on the immortal Model T and closed his plant to prepare for Model A. The Federal Reserve index of industrial production receded, presumably as a result of the Ford shutdown, and there was general talk of depression. The effect on the market was imperceptible. At the end of the year, by which time production had also turned up again, the *Times* industrials had reached 245, a net gain of 69 points for the year.

The year 1927 is historic from another point of view in the lore of the stock market. According to a long-accepted doctrine, it was in this year that the seeds of the eventful disaster were sown. The responsibility rests with an act of generous but ill-advised internationalism. Some – including Mr Hoover – have thought it almost disloyal, although in those days accusations of treason were still made with some caution.

In 1925, under the aegis of the then Chancellor of the Exchequer, Mr Winston Churchill, Britain returned to the gold standard at the old or pre-World War I relationship between gold, dollars, and the pound. There is no doubt that Churchill was more impressed by the grandeur of the traditional, or $4·86, pound than by the more subtle consequences of overvaluation, which he is widely assumed not to have understood. The consequences, nonetheless, were real and severe. Customers of Britain had now to use these costly pounds to buy goods at prices that still reflected wartime inflation. Britain was, accordingly, an unattractive place for foreigners to buy. For the same reason it was an easy place in which to sell. In 1925 began the long series of exchange crises which, like the lions in Trafalgar Square and the street walkers in Piccadilly, are now an established part of the British scene. There were also unpleasant domestic consequences; the bad market for coal and the effort to reduce costs and prices to meet world competition led to the general strike in 1926.

Then, as since, gold when it escaped from Britain or Europe came to the United States. This might be discouraged if prices of goods were high and interest rates were low in this country. (The United States would be a poor place in which to buy and invest.) In the spring of 1927, three august pilgrims – Montagu Norman, the Governor of the Bank of England, the durable Hjalmar Schacht, then Governor of the Reichsbank, and Charles Rist, the Deputy Governor of the Bank of France – came to the United States to urge an easy money policy. (They had previously pleaded with success for a roughly similar policy in 1925.) The Federal Reserve obliged. The rediscount rate of the New York Federal Reserve Bank was cut from 4 to 3·5 per cent. Government securities were purchased in considerable volume with the mathematical consequence of leaving the banks and individuals who had sold them with money to spare. Adolph C. Miller, a dissenting member of the Federal Reserve Board, subsequently described this as 'the greatest and boldest operation ever undertaken by the Federal Reserve

System, and ... [it] resulted in one of the most costly errors committed by it or any other banking system in the last 75 years!'[1] The funds that the Federal Reserve made available were either invested in common stocks or (and more important) they became available to help finance the purchase of common stocks by others. So provided with funds, people rushed into the market. Perhaps the most widely read of all the interpretations of the period, that of Professor Lionel Robbins of the London School of Economics, concludes: 'From that date, according to all the evidence, the situation got completely out of control.'[2]

This view that the action of the Federal Reserve authorities in 1927 was responsible for the speculation and collapse which followed has never been seriously shaken. There are reasons why it is attractive. It is simple, and it exonerates both the American people and their economic system from any substantial blame. The danger of being guided by foreigners is well known, and Norman and Schacht had some special reputation for sinister motives.

Yet the explanation obviously assumes that people will always speculate if only they can get the money to finance it. Nothing could be further from the case. There were times before and there have been long periods since when credit was plentiful and cheap – far cheaper than in 1927-9 – and when speculation was negligible. Nor, as we shall see later, was speculation out of control after 1927, except that it was beyond the reach of men who did not want in the least to control it. The explanation is a tribute only to a recurrent preference, in economic matters, for formidable nonsense.

4

Until the beginning of 1928, even a man of conservative mind

1. Testimony before Senate Committee, quoted by Lionel Robbins, *The Great Depression*, New York (Macmillan), 1934, p. 53.
2. ibid., p. 53.

could believe that the prices of common stock were catching up with the increase in corporation earnings, the prospect for further increases, the peace and tranquillity of the times, and the certainty that the Administration then firmly in power in Washington would take no more than necessary of any earnings in taxes. Early in 1928, the nature of the boom changed. The mass escape into make-believe, so much a part of the true speculative orgy, started in earnest. It was still necessary to reassure those who required some tie, however tenuous, to reality. And, as will be seen presently, this process of reassurance – of inventing the industrial equivalents of the Florida climate – eventually achieved the status of a profession. However, the time had come, as in all periods of speculation, when men sought not to be persuaded of the reality of things but to find excuses for escaping into the new world of fantasy.

There were many indications by 1928 that this phase had come. Most obvious was the behaviour of the market. While the winter months of 1928 were rather quiet, thereafter the market began to rise, not by slow, steady steps, but by great vaulting leaps. On occasion it also came down the same way, only to recover and go higher again. In March 1928 the industrial average rose nearly 25 points. News of the boiling market was frequently on the front page. Individual issues sometimes made gains of 10, 15, and 20 points in a single day's trading. On 12 March, Radio, in many respects the speculative symbol of the time, gained 18 points. On the following day it opened 22 points above the previous close. Then it lost 20 points on the announcement that the behaviour of the trading in the stock was being investigated by the Exchange, gained 15 points, and fell off 9.[1] A few days later, on a strong market, it made another 18-point gain.

The March boom also celebrated, beyond anything theretofore, the operations of the big professional traders. The lore

1. Allen, op. cit., p. 297.

of competitive markets pictures the Stock Exchange as the most impersonal of markets. No doctrine is more jealously guarded by the prophets and defenders of the Stock Exchange. 'The Exchange is a market place where prices reflect the basic law of supply and demand,' the New York Stock Exchange says firmly of itself.[1] Yet even the most devout Wall Streeter allows himself on occasion to believe that more personal influences have a hand in his destiny. Somewhere around there are big men who put stocks up and put them down.

As the boom developed, the big men became more and more omnipotent in the popular or at least in the speculative view. In March, according to this view, the big men decided to put the market up, and even some serious scholars have been inclined to think that a concerted move catalysed this upsurge. If so, the important figure was John J. Raskob. Raskob had impressive associations. He was a director of General Motors, an ally of the Du Ponts, and soon to be Chairman of the Democratic National Committee by choice of Al Smith. A contemporary student of the market, Professor Charles Amos Dice of the Ohio State University, thought this latter appointment a particular indication of the new prestige of Wall Street and the esteem in which it was held by the American people. 'Today', he observed, 'the shrewd, worldly-wise candidate of one of the great political parties chooses one of the outstanding operators in the stock market ... as a goodwill creator and popular vote getter.'[2]

On 23 March 1928, on taking ship for Europe, Raskob spoke favourably of prospects for automobile sales for the rest of the year and the share in the business that General Motors would have. He may also have suggested – the evidence is not entirely

1. *Understanding the New York Stock Exchange*, 3rd ed, New York (Stock Exchange), April 1954, p. 2.
2. *New Levels in the Stock Market*, New York (McGraw-Hill), 1929, p. 9.

clear – that G.M. stock should be selling at not less than twelve times earnings. This would have meant a price of 225 as compared with a current quotation of about 187. Such, as the *Times* put it, was 'the magic of his name' that Mr Raskob's 'temperate bit of optimism' sent the market into a boiling fury. On 24 March, a Saturday, General Motors gained nearly 5 points, and the Monday following it went to 199. The surge in General Motors, meanwhile, set off a great burst of trading elsewhere in the list.

Among the others who were assumed to have put their strength behind the market that spring was William Crapo Durant. Durant was the organizer of General Motors, whom Raskob and the Du Ponts had thrown out of the company in 1920. After a further adventure in the auto business, he had turned to full-time speculation in the stock market. The seven Fisher brothers were also believed to be influential. They too were General Motors alumni and had come to Wall Street with the great fortune they had realized from the sale of the Fisher-body plants. Still another was Arthur W. Cutten, the Canadian-born grain speculator who had recently shifted his market operations to Wall Street from the Chicago Board of Trade. As a market operator, Cutten surmounted substantial personal handicaps. He was very hard of hearing, and some years later, before a congressional committee, even his own counsel conceded that his memory was very defective.

Observing this group as a whole Professor Dice was especially struck by their 'vision for the future and boundless hope and optimism'. He noted that 'they did not come into the market hampered by the heavy armour of tradition'. In recounting their effect on the market, Professor Dice obviously found the English language verging on inadequacy. 'Led by these mighty knights of the automobile industry, the steel industry, the radio industry . . .' he said, 'and finally joined, in despair, by many professional traders who, after much sackcloth and ashes, had caught the vision of progress, the Coolidge market had 'gone forward like the phalanxes of Cyrus, parasang upon parasang and again parasang upon parasang . . .'[1]

## 5

In June of 1928 the market retreated a parasang or two – in fact, the losses during the first three weeks were almost as great as the March gains. 12 June, a day of particularly heavy losses, was a landmark. For a year or more, men of vision had been saying that the day might come when five million shares would be traded on the New York Stock Exchange. Once this had been only a wild conversational gambit, but for some time it had shown signs of being overtaken by the reality. On 12 March, the volume of trading had reached 3,875,910 shares, an all-time high. By the end of the month such a volume had become commonplace. On 27 March, 4,790,270 shares were traded. Then on 12 June, 5,052,790 shares changed hands. The ticker also fell nearly two hours behind the market; Radio dropped 23 points, and a New York paper began its accounts of the day's events; 'Wall Street's bull market collapsed yesterday with a detonation heard round the world.'

The announcement of the death of the bull market was as premature as any since that of the death of Mark Twain. In July there was a small net gain, and in August a strong upsurge. Thereafter not even the approach of the election caused serious hesitation. People remained unperturbed when, on 17 September, Roger W. Babson told an audience in Wellesley, Massachusetts, that if 'Smith should be elected with a Democratic Congress we are almost certain to have a resulting business depression in 1929'. He also said that 'the election of Hoover and a Republican Congress should result in continued prosperity for 1929', and it may have been that the public knew it

1. Op. cit., pp. 6–7.

would be Hoover. In any case, during the same month reassurance came from still higher authority. Andrew W. Mellon said, 'There is no cause for worry. The high tide of prosperity will continue.'

Mr Mellon did not know. Neither did any of the other public figures who then, as since, made similar statements. These are not forecasts; it is not to be supposed that the men who make them are privileged to look further into the future than the rest. Mr Mellon was participating in a ritual which, in our society, is thought to be of great value for influencing the course of the business cycle. By affirming solemnly that prosperity will continue, it is believed, one can help insure that prosperity will in fact continue. Especially among businessmen the faith in the efficiency of such incantation is very great.

6

Hoover was elected in a landslide. This, were the speculators privy to Mr Hoover's mind, should have caused a heavy fall in the market. In his memoirs Mr Hoover states that as early as 1925 he became concerned over the 'growing tide of speculation'.[1] During the months and years that followed this concern gradually changed to alarm, and then to something only slightly less than a premonition of total disaster. 'There are crimes', Mr Hoover said of speculation, 'far worse than murder for which men should be reviled and punished.'[2] As Secretary of Commerce he had sought nothing so much as to get the market under control.

Mr Hoover's attitude toward the market was, however, an exceptionally well-kept secret. People did not know of his efforts, uniformly frustrated by Coolidge and the Federal

1. *The Memoirs of Herbert Hoover: The Great Depression, 1929–1941*, New York (Macmillan), 1952, p. 5.
2. ibid., p. 14.

Reserve Board, to translate his thoughts into action. The news of his election, so far from causing a panic, set off the greatest increase in buying to date. On 7 November, the day after the election, there was a 'victory boom', and the market leaders climbed 5 to 15 points. Volume reached 4,894,670 shares, or only a little less than the all-time record of 12 June, and this new level was reached on a rising, not a falling market. On 16 November, a further wave of buying hit the market. An astonishing 6,641,250 shares changed hands – far above the previous record. The *Times* industrial averages made a net gain of 4½ points on the day's trading – then considered an impressive advance. Apart from the afterglow of the election, there was nothing particular to incite this enthusiasm. The headlines of the day told only of the sinking of the steamship *Vestris* and the epic achievements of the officers and crew in shouldering aside the women and children and saving their own lives. 20 November was another huge day. Trading – 6,503,230 shares – was fractionally smaller than on the sixteenth, but by common agreement it was much more frantic. The following morning the *Times* observed that 'for cyclonic violence yesterday's stock market has never been exceeded in the history of Wall Street'.

December was not so good. Early in the month there was a bad break, and, on 8 December, Radio fell a ghastly 72 points in one day. However, the market steadied and then came back. Over the whole year of 1928 the *Times* industrial average gained 86 points, or from 245 to 331. During the year Radio went from 85 to 420 (it had never paid a dividend); Du Pont went from 310 to 525; Montgomery Ward from 117 to 440; Wright Aeronautic from 69 to 289.[1] During the year 920,550,032 shares were traded on the New York Stock Exchange, as compared with a record-breaking 576,990,875 in 1927.[2] But there was still another and even more significant index of what was

1. Dice, op. cit., p. 11.
2. *Year Book, 1929–1930*, New York (Stock Exchange).

happening in the market. That was the phenomenal increase in trading on margin.

## 7

As noted, at some point in the growth of a boom all aspects of property ownership become irrelevant except the prospect for an early rise in price. Income from the property, or enjoyment of its use, or even its long-run worth are now academic. As in the case of the more repulsive Florida lots, these usufructs may be non-existent or even negative. What is important is that tomorrow or next week market values will rise – as they did yesterday or last week – and a profit can be realized.

It follows that the only reward to ownership in which the boomtime owner has an interest is the increase in values. Could the right to the increased value be somehow divorced from the other and now unimportant fruits of possession and also from as many as possible of the burdens of ownership, this would be much welcomed by the speculator. Such an arrangement would enable him to concentrate on speculation which, after all, is the business of a speculator.

Such is the genius of capitalism that where a real demand exists it does not go long unfilled. In all great speculative orgies devices have appeared to enable the speculator so to concentrate on his business. In the Florida boom the trading was in 'binders'. Not the land itself but the right to buy the land at a stated price was traded. This right to buy – which was obtained by a down payment of ten per cent of the purchase price – could be sold. It thus conferred on the speculators the full benefit of the increase in values. After the value of the lot had risen he could resell the binder for what he had paid plus the full amount of the increase in price.

The worst of the burdens of ownership, whether of land or any other asset, is the need to put up the cash represented by the purchase price. The use of the binder cut this burden by ninety per cent – or it multiplied tenfold the amount of acreage from which the speculator could harvest an increase in value. The buyer happily gave up the other advantages of ownership. These included the current income of which, invariably, there was none and the prospect of permanent use in which he had not the slightest interest.

The stock market also has its design for concentrating the speculative energies of the speculator, and, as might be expected, it improves substantially on the crudities of the real estate market. In the stock market the buyer of securities on margin gets full title to his property in an unconditional sale. But he rids himself of the most grievous burden of ownership – that of putting up the purchase price – by leaving his securities with his broker as collateral for the loan that paid for them. The buyer again gets the full benefit of any increase in value – the price of the securities goes up, but the loan that bought them does not. In the stock market the speculative buyer also gets the earnings of the securities he purchased. However, in the days of this history the earnings were almost invariably less than the interest that was paid on the loan. Often they were much less. Yields on securities regularly ranged from nothing to one or two per cent. Interest on the loans that carried them was often eight, ten, or more per cent. The speculator was willing to pay to divest himself of all of the usufructs of security ownership except the chance for capital gain.

The machinery by which Wall Street separates the opportunity to speculate from the unwanted returns and burdens of ownership is ingenious, precise, and almost beautiful. Banks supply funds to brokers, brokers to customers, and the collateral goes back to banks in a smooth and all but automatic flow. Margins – the cash which the speculator must supply in addition to the securities to protect the loan and which he must augment if the value of the collateral securities should fall and so lower the protection they provide – are effortlessly calculated and watched. The interest rate moves quickly and easily to keep the supply of funds adjusted to the demand. Wall Street, however, has never been able to express its pride in these arrangements. They are admirable and even wonderful only in relation to the purpose they serve. The purpose is to accommodate the speculator and facilitate speculation. But the purposes cannot be admitted. If Wall Street confessed this purpose, many thousands of moral men and women would have no choice but to condemn it for nurturing an evil thing and call for reform. Margin trading must be defended not on the grounds that it efficiently and ingeniously assists the speculator, but that it encourages the extra trading which changes a thin and anaemic market into a thick and healthy one. At best this is a dull by-product and a dubious one. Wall Street, in these matters, is like a lovely and accomplished woman who must wear black cotton stockings, heavy woollen underwear, and parade her knowledge as a cook because, unhappily, her supreme accomplishment is as a harlot.

However, even the most circumspect friend of the market would concede that the volume of brokers' loans – of loans collateralled by the securities purchased on margin – is a good index of the volume of speculation. Measured by this index, the amount of speculation was rising very fast in 1928. Early in the twenties the volume of brokers' loans – because of their liquidity they are often referred to as call loans or loans in the call market – varied from a billion to a billion and a half dollars. By early 1926 they had increased to two and a half billion and remained at about that level for most of the year. During 1927 there was another increase of about a billion dollars, and at the end of the year they reached $3,480,780,000. This was an incredible sum, but it was only the beginning. In the two dull winter months of 1928 there was a small decline and then expansion began in earnest. Brokers' loans reached four billion on the first of June 1928, five billion on the first of

November, and by the end of the year they were well along to six billion.[1] Never had there been anything like it before.

People were swarming to buy stocks on margin – in other words, to have the increase in price without the cost of ownership. This cost was being assumed, in the first instance, by the New York banks, but they, in turn, were rapidly becoming the agents for lenders the country over and even the world around. There is no mystery as to why so many wished to lend so much in New York. One of the paradoxes of speculation in securities is that the loans that underwrite it are among the safest of all investments. They are protected by stocks which under all ordinary circumstances are instantly saleable, and by a cash margin as well. The money, as noted, can be retrieved on demand. At the beginning of 1928 this admirably liquid and exceptionally secure outlet for non-risk capital was paying around five per cent. While five per cent is an excellent gilt-edged return, the rate rose steadily through 1928, and during the last week of the year it reached twelve per cent. This was still with complete safety.

In Montreal, London, Shanghai, and Hong Kong there was talk of these rates. Everywhere men of means told themselves that twelve per cent was twelve per cent. A great river of gold began to converge on Wall Street, all of it to help Americans hold common stock on margin. Corporations also found these rates attractive. At twelve per cent Wall Street might even provide a more profitable use for the working capital of a company than additional production. A few firms made this decision: instead of trying to produce goods with its manifold headaches and inconveniences, they confined themselves to financing speculation. Many more companies started lending their surplus funds on Wall Street.

1. The year-end figure was $5,722,258,724. Figures are from the New York Stock Exchange *Year Book, 1928–1929*, and do not include brokers' time loans.

There were still better ways of making money. In principle, New York banks could borrow money from the Federal Reserve Bank at five per cent and re-lend it in the call market for twelve. In practice they did. This was, possibly, the most profitable arbitrage operation of all time.

## 8

However, there were many ways of making money in 1928. Never had there been a better time to get rich, and people knew it. 1928, indeed, was the last year in which Americans were buoyant, uninhibited, and utterly happy. It wasn't that 1928 was too good to last; it was only that it didn't last.

In the January issue of *World's Work*, Will Payne, after reflecting on the wonders of the year just over, went on to explain the difference between a gambler and an investor. A gambler, he pointed out, wins only because someone else loses. Where it is investment, all gain. One investor, he explained, buys General Motors at $100, sells it to another at $150, who sells it to a third at $200. Everyone makes money. As Walter Bagehot once observed: 'All people are most credulous when they are most happy.'[1]

1. *Lombard Street*, London (John Murray), 1922 ed., p. 151.

# CHAPTER III

# SOMETHING SHOULD BE DONE?

I

PURELY in retrospect it is easy to see how 1929 was destined to be a year to remember. This was not because Mr Hoover was soon to become President and had inimical intentions toward the market. Those intentions developed at least partly in retrospect. Nor was it because men of wisdom could tell that a depression was overdue. No one, wise or unwise, knew or now knows when depressions are due or overdue.

Rather, it was simply that a roaring boom was in progress in the stock market and, like all booms, it had to end. On the first of January 1929, as a simple matter of probability, it was most likely that the boom would end before the year was out, with a diminishing chance that it would end in any given year thereafter. When prices stopped rising – when the supply of people who were buying for an increase was exhausted – then ownership on margin would become meaningless and everyone would want to sell. The market wouldn't level out; it would fall precipitately.

All this being so, the position of the people who had at least nominal responsibility for what was going on was a complex one. One of the oldest puzzles of politics is who is to regulate the regulators. But an equally baffling problem, which has never received the attention it deserves, is who is to make wise those who are required to have wisdom.

Some of those in positions of authority wanted the boom to continue. They were making money out of it, and they may have had an intimation of the personal disaster which awaited them when the boom came to an end. But there were also some who saw, however dimly, that a wild speculation was in progress and that something should be done. For these people, however, every proposal to act raised the same intractable problem. The consequences of successful action seemed almost as terrible as the consequences of inaction, and they could be more horrible for those who took the action.

A bubble can easily be punctured. But to incise it with a needle so that it subsides gradually is a task of no small delicacy. Among those who sensed what was happening in early 1929, there was some hope but no confidence that the boom could be made to subside. The real choice was between an immediate and deliberately engineered collapse and a more serious disaster later on. Someone would certainly be blamed for the ultimate collapse when it came. There was no question whatever as to who would be blamed should the boom be deliberately deflated. (For nearly a decade the Federal Reserve authorities had been denying their responsibility for the deflation of 1920–1.) The eventual disaster also had the inestimable advantage of allowing a few more days, weeks, or months of life. One may doubt if at any time in early 1929 the problem was ever framed in terms of quite such stark alternatives. But however disguised or evaded, these were the choices which haunted every serious conference on what to do about the market.

2

The men who had responsibility for these ineluctable choices were the President of the United States, the Secretary of the Treasury, the Federal Reserve Board in Washington, and the Governor and Directors of the Federal Reserve Bank of New York. As the most powerful of the Federal Reserve Banks, and the one with the market at its doorstep, the New York bank both had and assumed responsibilities which were not accepted by the other eleven banks of the system.

President Coolidge neither knew nor cared what was going on. A few days before leaving office in 1929, he cheerily observed that things were 'absolutely sound' and that stocks were 'cheap at current prices'[1]. In earlier years, whenever warned that speculation was getting out of hand, he had comforted himself with the thought that this was the primary responsibility of the Federal Reserve Board.[2] The Board was a semi-autonomous body precisely because Congress wanted to protect it from excessive political interference by the Executive.

However tender his scruples, President Coolidge could have acted through his Secretary of the Treasury, who served, ex-officio, as a member of the Federal Reserve Board. The Secretary also had the primary responsibility for economic and especially for financial policy. But on this as on other matters of economic policy, the incumbent, Andrew W. Mellon, was a passionate advocate of inaction. The responsibility thus passed to the Federal Reserve Board and the Federal Reserve Banks.

The regulation of economic activity is without doubt the most inelegant and unrewarding of public endeavours. Almost everyone is opposed to it in principle; its justification always relies on the unprepossessing case for the lesser evil. Regulation originates in raucous debate in Congress in which the naked interests of pressure groups may at times involve an exposure bordering on the obscene. Promulgation and enforcement of rules and regulations is by grinding bureaucracies which are ceaselessly buffeted by criticism. In recent times it has become obligatory for the regulators at every opportunity to confess their inadequacy, which in any case is all too evident.

The great exception to this dreary story is the regulatory activity of the central bank – with us, the Federal Reserve System. Here is regulation of a seemly and becoming sort. No

1. *The Memoirs of Herbert Hoover*, p. 16.
2. ibid., p. 11.

one apologizes for it; men of impeccable conservatism would rise to espouse such regulation were they called upon to do so, which they almost never are. This regulation is not the work of thousands of clerks, statisticians, hearing officers, lawyers, and lesser beings in a teeming office building on the Mall. Rather it emerges in the measured and orderly discussion of men of quiet and dignified mien, each at his accustomed place around a handsome table in a richly panelled and richly draperied room. These men do not issue orders; at most they suggest. Chiefly they move interest rates, buy or sell securities and, in doing so, nudge the economy here and restrain it there. Because the meanings of their actions are not understood by the great majority of the people, they can reasonably be assumed to have superior wisdom. Their actions will on occasion be criticized. More often they will be scrutinized for hidden meanings.

Such is the mystique of central banking. Such was the awe-inspiring role in 1929 of the Federal Reserve Board in Washington, the policy-making body which guided and directed the twelve Federal Reserve Banks. However, there was a jarring difficulty. The Federal Reserve Board in those times was a body of startling incompetence.

For several years, until late in 1927, the Chairman and guiding genius presumptive was one Daniel R. Crissinger. He had been trained for his task by serving as General Counsel of the Marion Steam Shovel Company of Marion, Ohio. There is no indication that he was an apt student. However, his background seemed satisfactory to another Marion boy, Warren G. Harding, who had brought him to Washington, where he was regarded as a hack politician from Ohio. In 1927 Crissinger was replaced by Roy A. Young, who for eight years had been Governor of the Minneapolis Federal Reserve Bank. Young, a more substantial figure, was undoubtedly aware of what was going on. However, he was a man of caution who sought no fame as a martyr to the broken boom. His colleagues were among the more commonplace of Harding–Coolidge appointees. With one exception – the erstwhile college professor Adolph C. Miller – they have been conservatively described by Herbert Hoover as 'mediocrities'.[1]

The New York Federal Reserve Bank was under more vigorous leadership. For several years, until 1928, its governor had been Benjamin Strong, the first American since Nicholas Biddle to make an important reputation as a central banker. Strong's views were regarded throughout the System with only little less awe than the gold standard. However, in the view of Herbert Hoover – and in this instance Hoover's views are widely shared – Strong, so far from being concerned about the inflation, was the man most responsible for it. It was he who took the lead in 1927 in easing money rates to help the hard-pressed Europeans. For this Mr Hoover later called him 'a mental annex to Europe'.[2]

This is unfair. Governor Strong's action was entirely reasonable in the circumstances and, as noted in the last chapter, it takes more to start a speculation than a general ability to borrow money. Still, the New York Federal Reserve Bank, under Governor Strong's leadership, may not have been sufficiently perturbed by the speculation a block or two away. Nor was it after Governor Strong died in October 1928 and was replaced by George L. Harrison. A reason, no doubt, was the reassurance provided by people in high places who were themselves speculating heavily. One such was Charles E. Mitchell, the Chairman of the Board of the National City Bank, who on 1 January 1929 became a class A director of the Federal Reserve Bank of New York. The end of the boom would mean the end of Mitchell. He was not a man to expedite his own demise.

1. *The Memoirs of Herbert Hoover*, p. 9.
2. ibid., pp. 9, 10.

3

.In the accepted history of these times, the Federal Reserve authorities are held to be not so much unaware or unwilling as impotent. They would have liked to stop the boom, but they lacked the means. This puts far too elaborate a face on matters. And it largely disguises the real nature of the dilemma which the authorities faced.

The classic instruments of control were indeed largely useless. These, as almost every college sophomore knows, are two: open market operations and the manipulation of the rediscount rate. Open market sales of government securities[1] by the Federal Reserve bring to the vaults of the Reserve Banks the cash which is paid for the securities. There it remains sterile and harmless. Had it stayed in the commercial banks it would have been loaned to the public in multiple volume and particularly in those days to people who were buying common stocks.

If such a policy is to succeed, the Federal Reserve System rather obviously must have securities to sell. One of the inestimable blessings of the years of depression, war, and deficit-financing since 1930 is a spacious inventory of government debt in the Reserve Banks. In 1929 the Banks were not so well endowed. At the beginning of 1928, holdings were $617 million. During the first half of the year there were heavy sales as part of an effort to dry up the supply of funds that was feeding the market. Although sales were discontinued in the latter part of the year in the highly erroneous belief that the policy had succeeded and that the boom was under control, they couldn't have been continued much longer in any case. By the end of 1928 the inventory of government securities of the Federal Reserve System amounted only to $228 million. Had these all been dropped into the market, they might

1. Or the sale or reduction in inventory of commercial paper.

possibly have had some effect. But the Board was not given to any such drastic behaviour which, incidentally, would also have largely denuded the Reserve Banks of earning assets. Sales were made a few millions at a time in the early months of 1929, but the effect was inconsequential. Moreover, even in following this feeble policy the Board worried lest, in denying funds to the stock market, it might put a pinch on 'legitimate' business. The Reserve Banks continued to buy acceptances – the security that emerges in the course of financing ordinary non-speculative trade – and, relieved of the need to carry this paper, the commercial banks happily loaned more money in the stock market.

The other instrument of Federal Reserve policy was the rediscount rate. This is the rate at which member commercial banks borrow from the Reserve Banks of their district so that they may accommodate more borrowers than their own resources permit. In January 1929, the rediscount rate at the New York Federal Reserve Bank was five per cent. The rate on brokers' loans ranged from six to twelve per cent. Only a drastic increase would have made it unprofitable for a bank to borrow at the Federal Reserve in order to lend the proceeds, directly or indirectly, in the stock market. Apart from the general aversion to drastic action, such an increase would also have raised rates to ordinary businessmen, consumers, and farmers. In fact, higher interest rates would have been distressing to everyone but the speculator. A man who paid, say, an average of ten per cent to carry his holdings of Radio through 1928 would not have been either deterred or much disturbed had the rate been twice that high. During the same year, he made 500 per cent on the appreciation in the value of his investment.

On 14 February 1929, the New York Federal Reserve Bank proposed that the rediscount rate be raised from five to six per cent to check speculation. The Federal Reserve Board in

Washington thought this a meaningless gesture which would
only increase rates to business borrowers. A long controversy
ensued in which President Hoover sided with the Board against
the Bank. The rate was not increased until late in the summer.

There was another circumstance which gave the Reserve
authorities an admirable excuse for inaction. That was the
previously noted flow of funds from corporations and individuals to the market. During 1929, Standard Oil of New Jersey
contributed a daily average of $69 million to the call market;
Electric Bond and Share averaged over $100 million.[1] A few
corporations – Cities Service was one – even sold securities and
loaned the proceeds in the stock market.[2] By early 1929, loans
from these non-banking sources were approximately equal to
those from the banks. Later they became much greater. The
Federal Reserve authorities took for granted that they had no
influence whatever over this supply of funds.

4

In fact, the Federal Reserve was helpless only because it
wanted to be. Had it been determined to do something, it could
for example have asked Congress for authority to halt trading
on margin by granting the Board the power to set margin
requirements. Margins were not low in 1929; a residue of
caution had caused most brokers to require customers to put
up forty-five to fifty per cent of the value of the stocks they
were buying in cash. However, this was all the cash numerous
of their customers had. An increase in margins to, say, seventy-
five per cent in January 1929, or even a serious proposal to do
so, would have caused many small speculators and quite a few

1. *Stock Exchange Practices*, Report of the Committee on Banking
and Currency pursuant to Senate Resolution 84, Washington, 1934,
p. 16.

2. ibid., pp. 13–14.

big ones to sell. The boom would have come to a sudden and perhaps spectacular end. (The power to fix margin requirements was eventually given to the Federal Reserve Board by the Securities Exchange Act in 1934, a year in which the danger of a revival of speculation about equalled that of a renascence of prohibition.)

Actually, not even new legislation, or the threat of it, was needed. In 1929, a robust denunciation of speculators and speculation by someone in high authority and a warning that the market was too high would almost certainly have broken the spell. It would have brought some people back from the world of make-believe. Those who were planning to stay in the market as long as possible but still get out (or go short) in time would have got out or gone short. Their occupational nervousness could readily have been translated into an acute desire to sell. Once the selling started, some more vigorously voiced pessimism could easily have kept it going.

The very effectiveness of such a measure was the problem. Of all the weapons in the Federal Reserve arsenal, words were the most unpredictable in their consequences. Their effect might be sudden and terrible. Moreover, these consequences could be attributed with the greatest of precision to the person or persons who uttered the words. Retribution would follow. To the more cautious of the Federal Reserve officials in the early part of 1929 silence seemed literally golden.

Yet the boom was continuing. In January the *Times* industrials gained 30 points, more than during the post-election spree in November. Brokers' loans went up a whopping $260 million; on five different days, three of them as the market got off to a boiling start right after New Year, trading on the New York Exchange exceeded the magic five-million mark. Effective action would be disastrous; yet some action seemed unavoidable. Finally the Board decided to write a letter and issue a press release. It could do no less.

On 2 February, it addressed the individual Reserve Banks as follows:

A member [commercial bank] is not within its reasonable claims for re-discount facilities at its reserve bank when it borrows either for the purpose of making speculative loans or for the purpose of maintaining speculative loans. The board has no disposition to assume authority to interfere with the loan practices of member banks, so long as they do not involve the Federal reserve banks. It has, however, a grave responsibility whenever there is evidence that member banks are maintaining speculative security loans with the aid of Federal reserve credit.[1]

On 7 February, in what may be an even finer example of fiduciary prose – connoisseurs will wish to read it backward as well as forward – the Board warned the public:

When [the Board] finds that conditions are arising which obstruct the Federal reserve banks in the effective discharge of their functions of so managing the credit facilities of the Federal reserve system as to accommodate commerce and business, it is its duty to inquire into them and to take such measures as may be deemed suitable and effective in the circumstances to correct them; which, in the immediate situation, means to restrain the use, either directly or indirectly, of Federal Reserve facilities in aid of the growth of speculative credit.[2]

Almost simultaneously with this warning came the news that the Bank of England was raising the bank rate from four and one-half to five and one-half per cent in an effort to diminish the flow of British funds to the new Golconda. The result was a sharp break in the market. On 7 February, in a five-million share day, the *Times* industrials dropped 11 points, with a further drop on the day following. Thereafter the market recovered, but, for February as a whole, there was no appreciable net gain. Economists have long had a phrase for this

1. Thomas Wilson, *Fluctuations in Income and Employment*, p. 147.
2. ibid., pp. 147–8.

action – it was called the Federal Reserve's effort at 'moral suasion'. Since the market was only temporarily checked, there has been ever since virtually complete agreement that moral suasion was a failure.

Precisely the opposite conclusion could and probably should have been drawn. It is impossible to imagine a milder, more tentative, more palpably panic-striken communiqué than that issued by the Board. The statement that the Board had no intention of interfering with loans to support speculation so long as Federal Reserve credit was not involved is especially noteworthy. Clearly the Federal Reserve was less interested in checking speculation than in detaching itself from responsibility for the speculation that was going on. And it will be observed that some anonymous draughtsman achieved a wording which indicated that not the present level but only a further growth in speculation would be viewed with alarm. Yet in the then state of nervousness even these almost incredibly feeble words caused a sharp setback.

5

The nervousness of the market and the unsuspected moral authority of the equally nervous men of the Federal Reserve was even better illustrated in March. As the new month approached, Mr Coolidge made his blithe observation about stocks being cheap and the country being sound. The market surged up in what the papers dubbed 'The Inaugural Market', and on 4 March, his attitude towards speculators still unknown, Mr Hoover took over. The market for the next couple of weeks remained strong.

Then toward the end of the month disquieting news reached Wall Street. The Federal Reserve Board was meeting daily in Washington. It issued no statements. Newspapermen pressed the members after the sessions and were met with what then,

as now, was known as tight-lipped silence. There was not a
hint as to what the meetings were about, although everyone
knew they concerned the market. The meetings continued day
after day, and there was also an unprecedented Saturday
session.

Soon it was too much. On Monday, 25 March, the first
market day following the unseemly Saturday meeting, the
tension became unbearable. Although, or rather because,
Washington was still silent, people began to sell. Speculative
favourites – Commercial Solvents, Wright Aero, American
Railway Express – dropped 10 or 12 points or more; the *Times*
industrial average was off $9\frac{1}{2}$ points for the day. More important, some banks decided that, in the event of a Federal
Reserve crackdown, virtue might have a reward above revenue.
They began curtailing their loans in the call market, and the
rate on brokers' loans went to fourteen per cent.

On the next day, Tuesday, 26 March, everything was much
worse. The Federal Reserve Board was still maintaining its by
now demoralizing silence. A wave of fear swept the market.
More people decided to sell, and they sold in astonishing
volume. An amazing 8,246,740 shares changed hands on the
New York Stock Exchange, far above any previous record.
Prices seemed to drop vertically. At the low for the day 20- and
30-point losses were commonplace. The *Times* industrials at
one time were 15 points below the previous day's close. Thousands of speculators, in whose previous experience the market
had always risen, now saw for the first time the seamy side of
their new way of life. Each new quotation was far below the
last one. Moreover, the ticker, unable to cope with the unprecedented volume, was far behind the market. Not only were
things bad, but they had almost certainly become worse, yet
one couldn't tell from the ticker how much worse. Before the
day was out many of these thousands received a peremptory
telegram from their brokers – a telegram that was in the

starkest of contrast with the encouraging, half-confidential, rich-uncle tone of all previous communications. It asked more margin promptly.

Meanwhile the banks continued to trim sails for the storm. It is probable that some professional traders were selling because they foresaw the moment when there would be no money with which to carry stocks on margin. And that moment might be near, for on the morning of 26 March, the rate on call money reached twenty per cent, its high for the 1929 boom.

26 March 1929 could have been the end. Money could have remained tight. The authorities might have remained firm in their intention to keep it so. The panic might have continued. Each fall in prices would have forced a new echelon of speculators to sell, and so forced prices down still more. It did not happen, and if any man can be credited with this, the credit belongs to Charles E. Mitchell. The Federal Reserve authorities were ambivalent, but Mitchell was not. He was for the boom. Moreover, his prestige as head of one of the two largest and most influential commercial banks, his reputation as an aggressive and highly successful investment banker, and his position as a director of the New York Federal Reserve Bank meant that he spoke with at least as much authority as anyone in Washington. During the day, as money tightened, rates rose, and the market fell, Mitchell decided to take a hand. He told the press, 'We feel that we have an obligation which is paramount to any Federal Reserve warning, or anything else, to avert any dangerous crisis in the money market.' The National City, he said, would loan money as necessary to prevent liquidation. It would also (and did) borrow money from the New York Federal Reserve Bank to do what the Federal Reserve Bank had warned against doing. Disguised only slightly by the prose form of finance, Mitchell issued the Wall Street counterpart of Mayor Hague's famous manifesto, 'I am the law in Jersey City.'

Mitchell's words were like magic. By the end of trading on the 26th money rates had eased, and the market had rallied. The Federal Reserve remained silent, but now its silence was reassuring. It meant that it conceded Mitchell's mastery. The next day the National City regularized its commitment to the boom: it announced that it would insure reasonable interest rates by putting $25 million into the call market – $5 million when the rate was sixteen per cent, and $5 million additional for each percentage point. In its monthly letter a few days later, the bank justified its position and, incidentally, gave an admirable statement of the dilemma which the Federal Reserve faced. (The National City was in no doubt which horn of the dilemma it preferred.) The letter said: 'The National City Bank fully recognizes the dangers of overspeculation [sic] and endorses the desire of the Federal Reserve authorities to restrain excessive credit expansion for this purpose. At the same time, the bank, business generally, and it may be assumed the Federal Reserve Banks ... wish to avoid a general collapse of the securities markets such as would have a disastrous effect on business.'[1]

6

Mitchell did not escape criticism. A Senate investigation was mentioned. Senator Carter Glass, who as the sponsor of the Federal Reserve legislation had a keen proprietary interest in its operation, said: 'He avows his superior obligation to a frantic stock market over against the obligation of his oath as a director of the New York Federal Reserve Bank ... the Bank should ask for [his] immediate resignation.' That the Federal Reserve Board never dreamed of doing any such thing may be taken as a further indication that its moral suasion was being administered with a very infirm touch.

1. Quoted by Mitchell in *Stock Exchange Practices*, Hearings, Subcommittee, Senate Committee on Banking and Currency – The Pecora Committee, February–March 1933, Pt 6, p. 1817.

And the Federal Reserve was criticized even more than Mitchell – even though it could hardly have done less than it did. Arthur Brisbane said judiciously: 'If buying and selling stocks is wrong the government should close the Stock Exchange. If not, the Federal Reserve should mind its own business.' In a leading article in *Barron's*, a Mr Seth Axley was less even-handed: 'For the Federal Reserve Board to deny investors the means of recognizing economies which are now proved, skill which is now learned, and inventions which are almost unbelievable seems to justify doubt whether it is adequately interpreting the times.'[1] Since the principal action which the Federal Reserve had taken against investors had been to hold meetings and maintain silence, this was doubtless a trifle harsh. However, it was positively kind as compared with the words of a young Princeton scholar who emerged at this time as a leading defender of Wall Street.

Joseph Stagg Lawrence's book *Wall Street and Washington*, when it appeared later in the year bearing the distinguished imprimatur of the Princeton University Press, was described by a leading financial journal as a 'breath of fresh air'. The regulatory concern of the Federal Reserve about Wall Street, Mr Lawrence said in this remarkable volume, was motivated strictly by bias – a bias 'founded upon a clash of interests and a moral and intellectual antipathy between the wealthy, cultured, and conservative settlements on the seacoast [including Wall Street] and the poverty-stricken, illiterate, and radical pioneer communities of the interior'.[2] The cultured and conservative Mr Lawrence also had hard words for the defenders of the Federal Reserve in the Senate, including, oddly enough, the seaboard senator from Virginia, Carter Glass. 'It seems incredible that in the year of Our Grace 1929 a body of

1. *Barron's*, 6 May 1929.
2. *Wall Street and Washington*, Princeton (Princeton University Press), 1929, p. 3.

presumably intelligent public men should permit fanatical passions and provincial ignorance to find expression in unrestrained virulence. Yet this is precisely what has taken place . . . When the Senator from the Old Dominion rose in that chamber of absurdities, sometimes referred to as a deliberative assembly, his remarks were characterized by neither reason nor restraint. Blatant bigotry and turbulent provincialism have joined to condemn an innocent community.'[1] Some hardened Wall Streeters may have been surprised when they realized that the 'innocent community' meant them.

## 7

After the defeat by Mitchell in March, the Federal Reserve retired from the field. There continued to be some slight anxiety as to what it might do. In April, William Crapo Durant is supposed to have paid a secret night visit to the White House to warn President Hoover that if the Board were not called off it would precipate a terrible crash. The President was noncommittal, and Durant is said to have reduced his holdings before leaving on a trip to Europe.[2] In June from Princeton Mr Lawrence said that the Board was still 'doing its utmost to cast the proverbial monkey wrench into the machinery of prosperity'. He warned the Board that it had 'aroused the enmity of an honest, intelligent, and public-spirited community'.[3] (This also was Wall Street.) But the Board, in fact, had decided to leave that honest, intelligent, and public-spirited community strictly to its own devices. It realized,

1. *Wall Street and Washington*, Princeton (Princeton University Press), 1929, p. v.

2. The visit is described by Earl Sparling, *Mystery Men of Wall Street*, New York (Greenberg), 1930, pp. 3–8. The authority is dubious, although the author's facts, as distinct from his interpretation, are frequently accurate.

3. *Barron's*, 10 June 1929.

Governor Young said subsequently, that 'while the hysteria might be somewhat restrained', it would have to run its course, and the Reserve Banks could only brace themselves for the 'inevitable collapse'.[1] More accurately, the Federal Reserve authorities had decided not to be responsible for the collapse.

In August the Board finally agreed to an increase in the rediscount rate to six per cent. The market weakened only for a day. Any conceivable consequence of the action was nullified by a simultaneous easing of the buying rate on acceptances.

In fact, from the end of March on, the market had nothing further to fear from authority. President Hoover did ask Henry M. Robinson, a Los Angeles banker, to proceed as his emissary to New York and talk to the bankers there about the boom. According to Mr Hoover, Robinson was assured that things were sound.[2] Richard Whitney, the Vice-President of the Exchange, was also summoned to the White House and told that something should be done about speculation. Nothing was done, and Mr Hoover was able to find some solace in the thought that primary responsibility for regulating the Stock Exchange rested with the Governor of New York, Franklin D. Roosevelt.[3]

Roosevelt, too, was following a *laissez-faire* policy, at least on the matter of the stock market. A firm of investment counsellors in Boston, called McNeel's Financial Service, describing itself with a deft Back Bay touch as 'An Aristocracy of Successful Investors', advertised a new guide to investment. The headline read: 'He made $70,000 after reading *Beating*

1. Seymour E. Harris, *Twenty Years of Federal Reserve Policy*, Cambridge (Harvard University Press), 1933, p. 547. I have made use of this ultra-conservative but very careful account of Federal Reserve policy.

2. Hoover, *Memoirs*, p. 17.

3. ibid. Mr Hoover, who is careless of such details, including his dates, describes Whitney as President of the Exchange, which he only later became.

*the Stock Market.*' No doubt whoever it was did. He might have made it without reading the volume or without being able to read. For now, free at last from all threat of government reaction or retribution, the market sailed off into the wild blue yonder. Especially after 1 June all hesitation disappeared. Never before or since have so many become so wondrously, so effortlessly, and so quickly rich. Perhaps Messrs Hoover and Mellon and the Federal Reserve were right in keeping their hands off. Perhaps it was worth being poor for a long time to be so rich for just a little while.

# CHAPTER IV

# IN GOLDMAN, SACHS WE TRUST

I

THE recondite problems of Federal Reserve policy were not the only questions that were agitating Wall Street intellectuals in the early months of 1929. There was worry that the country might be running out of common stocks. One reason prices of stocks were so high, it was explained, was that there weren't enough to go around, and, accordingly, they had acquired a 'scarcity value'. Some issues, it was said, were becoming so desirable that they would soon be taken out of the market and would not reappear at any price.

If, indeed, common stocks were becoming scarce it was in spite of as extraordinary a response of supply to demand as any in the history of that well-worn relationship. Without doubt, the most striking feature of the financial era which ended in the autumn of 1929 was the desire of people to buy securities and the effect of this on values. But the increase in the number of securities to buy was hardly less striking. And the ingenuity and zeal with which companies were devised in which securities might be sold was as remarkable as anything.

Not all of the increase in the volume of securities in 1928 and 1929 was for the sole purpose of accommodating the speculator. It was a good time to raise money for general corporate purposes. Investors would supply capital with enthusiasm and without tedious questions. (Seaboard Air Line was a speculative favourite of the period in part because many supposed it to be an aviation stock with growth possibilities.) In these years of prosperity men with vision of still greater prosperity stretching on and on and forever, naturally saw the importance of being well provided with plant and working capital. This was no time to be niggardly.

Also, it was an age of consolidation, and each new merger required, inevitably, some new capital and a new issue of securities to pay for it. A word must be said about the merger movement of the twenties.

It was not the first such movement but, in many respects, it was the first of its kind. Just before and just after the turn of the century in industry after industry, small companies were combined into large ones. The United States Steel Corporation, International Harvester, International Nickel, American Tobacco, and numerous other of the great corporations trace to this period. In these cases the firms which were combined produced the same or related products for the same national market. The primary motivation in all but the rarest cases was to reduce, eliminate, or regularize competition. Each of the new giants dominated an industry, and henceforth exercised measurable control over prices and production, and perhaps also over investment and the rate of technological innovation.

A few such mergers occurred in the twenties. Mostly, however, the mergers of this period brought together not firms in competition with each other but firms doing the same thing in different communities. Local electric, gas, water, bus, and milk companies were united in great regional or national systems. The purpose was not to eliminate competition, but rather the incompetence, somnambulance, naïveté, or even the unwarranted integrity of local managements. In the twenties, a man in downtown New York or Chicago could take unabashed pride in the fact that he was a financial genius. The local owners and managers were not. There was no false modesty when it came to citing the advantages of displacing yokels with a central management of decent sophistication.

In the case of utilities the instrument for accomplishing this

centralization of management and control was the holding
company. These bought control of the operating companies.
On occasion they bought control of other holding companies
which controlled yet other holding companies, which in turn,
directly or indirectly through yet other holding companies,
controlled the operating companies. Everywhere local power,
gas, and water companies passed into the possession of a
holding-company system.

Food retailing, variety stores, department stores, and motion
picture theatres showed a similar, although not precisely
identical, development. Here, too, local ownership gave way to
central direction and control. The instrument of this centralization, however, was not the holding company but the corporate
chain. These, more often than not, instead of taking over
existing businesses, established new outlets.

The holding companies issued securities in order to buy
operating properties, and the chains issued securities in order
to build new stores and theatres. While in the years before
1929 the burgeoning utility systems – Associated Gas and
Electric, Commonwealth and Southern, and the Insull companies – attracted great attention, the chains were at least as
symbolic of the era. Montgomery Ward was one of the prime
speculative favourites of the period; it owned its eminence to
the fact that it was a chain and thus had a particularly bright
future. The same was true of Woolworth, American Stores,
and others. Interest in branch and chain banking was also
strong, and it was widely felt that state and federal laws were
an archaic barrier to a consolidation which would knit the
small-town and small-city banks into a few regional and
national systems. Various arrangements for defeating the
intent of law, most notably bank holding companies, were
highly regarded.

Inevitably promoters organized some new companies
merely to capitalize on the public interest in industries with

a new and wide horizon and provide securities to sell. Radio and aviation stocks were believed to have a particularly satisfactory prospect, and companies were formed which never had more than a prospect. In September 1929, an advertisement in the *Times* called attention to the impending arrival of television and said with considerable prescience that the 'commercial possibilities of this new art defy imagination'. The ad opined, somewhat less presciently, that sets would be in use in homes that fall. However, in the main, the market boom of 1929 was rooted directly or indirectly in existing industries and enterprises. New and fanciful issues for new and fanciful purposes, ordinarily so important in times of speculation, played a relatively small part. No significant amount of stock was sold in companies 'To Make Salt Water Fresh – For building of Hospitals for Bastard Children – For building of Ships against Pirates – For importing a Number of large Jack Asses from Spain', or even 'For a Wheel of Perpetual Motion', to cite a representative list of promotions at the time of the South Sea Bubble.[1]

2

The most notable piece of speculative architecture of the late twenties, and the one by which, more than any other device, the public demand for common stocks was satisfied, was the investment trust or company. The investment trust did not promote new enterprises or enlarge old ones. It merely arranged that people could own stock in old companies through the medium of new ones. Even in the United States, in the twenties, there were limits to the amount of real capital which existing enterprises could use or new ones could be created to employ. The virtue of the investment trust was that it brought about an almost complete divorce of the volume of corporate

1. Walter Bagehot, *Lombard Street*, pp. 130, 131.

securities outstanding from the volume of corporate assets in existence. The former could be twice, thrice, or any multiple of the latter. The volume of underwriting business and of securities available for trading on the exchanges all expanded accordingly. So did the securities to own, for the investment trusts sold more securities than they bought. The difference went into the call market, real estate, or the pockets of the promoters. It is hard to imagine an invention better suited to the time or one better designed to eliminate the anxiety about the possible shortage of common stocks.

The idea of the investment trust is an old one, although, oddly enough, it came late to the United States. Since the eighties in England and Scotland, investors, mostly smaller ones, had pooled their resources by buying stock in an investment company. The latter, in turn, invested the funds so secured. A typical trust held securities in from five hundred to a thousand operating companies. As a result, the man with a few pounds, or even a few hundred, was able to spread his risk far more widely than were he himself to invest. And the management of the trusts could be expected to have a far better knowledge of companies and prospects in Singapore, Madras, Capetown, and the Argentine, places to which British funds regularly found their way, than the widow in Bristol or the doctor in Glasgow. The smaller risk and better information well justified the modest compensation of those who managed the enterprise. Despite some early misadventures, the investment trusts soon became an established part of the British scene.

Before 1921 in the United States only a few small companies existed for the primary purpose of investing in the securities of other companies.[1] In that year, interest in invest-

[1] One estimate puts the number at about forty. Cf. *Investment Trusts and Investment Companies*, Pt I, Report of the Securities and Exchange Commission, Washington, 1939, p. 36

ment trusts began to develop, partly as the result of a number of newspaper and magazine articles describing the English and Scottish trusts. The United States, it was pointed out, had not been keeping abreast of the times; other countries were excelling us in fiduciary innovation. Soon, however, we began to catch up. More trusts were organized, and by the beginning of 1927 an estimated 160 were in existence. Another 140 were formed during that year.[1]

The managers of the British trusts normally enjoy the greatest of discretion in investing the funds placed at their disposal. At first the American promoters were wary of asking for such a vote of confidence. Many of the early trusts were trusts – the investor bought an interest in a specified assortment of securities which were then deposited with a trust company. At the least the promoters committed themselves to a rigorous set of rules on the kinds of securities to be purchased and the way they were to be held and managed. But as the twenties wore along, such niceties disappeared. The investment trust became, in fact, an investment corporation.[2] It sold its securities to the public – sometimes just common stock, more often common and preferred stock, debenture and mortgage bonds – and the proceeds were then invested as the management saw fit. Any possible tendency of the common stockholder to interfere with the management was prevented by selling him non-voting stock or having him assign his voting rights to a management-controlled voting trust.

For a long time the New York Stock Exchange looked with suspicion on the investment trusts; only in 1929 was listing permitted. Even then the Committee on the Stock List required an investment trust to post with the Exchange the book and

1. ibid., p. 36.

2. And would be more accurately described as an investment company or investment corporation. However, I have kept here to the less precise but more customary usage.

market value of the securities held at the time of listing and once a year thereafter to provide an inventory of its holdings. This provision confined the listing of most of the investment trusts to Curb, Boston, Chicago, or other road company exchanges. Apart from its convenience, this refusal to disclose was thought to be a sensible precaution. Confidence in the investment judgement of the managers of the trusts was very high. To reveal the stocks they were selecting might, it was said, set off a dangerous boom in the securities they favoured. Historians have told with wonder of one of the promotions at the time of the South Sea Bubble. It was 'For an Undertaking which shall in due time be revealed'. The stock is said to have sold exceedingly well. As promotions the investment trusts were, on the record, more wonderful. They were undertakings the nature of which was never to be revealed, and their stock also sold exceedingly well.

3

During 1928 an estimated 186 investment trusts were organized; by the early months of 1929 they were being promoted at the rate of approximately one each business day, and a total of 265 made their appearance during the course of the year. In 1927 the trusts sold to the public about $400,000,000 worth of securities; in 1929 they marketed an estimated three billions worth. This was at least a third of all the new capital issues in that year; by the autumn of 1929 the total assets of the investment trusts were estimated to exceed eight billions of dollars. They had increased approximately elevenfold since the beginning of 1927.[1]

The parthenogenesis of an investment trust differed from that of an ordinary corporation. In nearly all cases it was sponsored by another company, and by 1929 a surprising

1. The estimates in this paragraph are all from *Investment Trusts and Investment Companies*, Pt III, Chap. 1, pp. 3, 4.

number of different kinds of concerns were bringing the trusts into being. Investment banking houses, commercial banks, brokerage firms, securities dealers, and, most important, other investment trusts were busy giving birth to new trusts. The sponsors ranged in dignity from the House of Morgan, sponsor of the United and Alleghany Corporations, down to one Chauncey D. Parker, the head of a fiscally perilous investment banking firm in Boston, who organized three investment trusts in 1929 and sold $25,000,000 worth of securities to an eager public. Chauncey then lost most of the proceeds and lapsed into bankruptcy.[1]

Sponsorship of a trust was not without its rewards. The sponsoring firm normally executed a management contract with its offspring. Under the usual terms, the sponsor ran the investment trust, invested its funds, and received a fee based on a percentage of capital or earnings. Were the sponsor a Stock Exchange firm, it also received commissions on the purchase and sale of securities for its trust. Many of the sponsors were investment banking firms, which meant, in effect, that the firm was manufacturing securities it could then bring to market. This was an excellent way of insuring an adequate supply of business.

The enthusiasm with which the public sought to buy investment trust securities brought the greatest rewards of all. Almost invariably people were willing to pay a sizeable premium over the offering price. The sponsoring firm (or *its* promoters) received allotments of stock or warrants which entitled them to stock at the offering price. These they were then able to sell at once at a profit. Thus one of the enterprises of the Mr Chauncey D. Parker just mentioned – a company with the resounding name of Seaboard Utilities Shares Corporation – issued 1,600,000 shares of common stock on which the company netted $10.32 a share. That, however, was not the price

1. ibid., Pt III, Chap. 2, p. 37 ff.

paid by the public. It was the price at which the stock was issued to Parker and his colleagues. They in turn sold their shares to the public at from $11 to $18.25 and split the profit with the dealers who marketed the securities.[1]

Operations of this sort were not confined to the lowly or the vaguely disreputable. J. P. Morgan and Company, which (with Bonbright and Company) sponsored United Corporation in January 1929, offered a package of one share of common stock and one of preferred to a list of friends, Morgan partners included, at $75. This was a bargain. When trading in United Corporation began a week later, the price was 92 bid, 94 asked on the over-the-counter market, and after four days the stock reached 99. Stock that had been taken up at 75 could be and was promptly resold at these prices.[2] That such agreeable incentives greatly stimulated the organization of new investment trusts is hardly surprising.

## 4

There were some, indeed, who only regretted that everyone could not participate in the gains from these new engines of financial progress. One of those who had benefited from the United Corporation promotion just mentioned was John J. Raskob. As Chairman of the Democratic National Committee, he was also politically committed to a firm friendship for the people. He believed that everyone should be in on the kind of opportunities he himself enjoyed.

One of the fruits of this generous impulse during the year was an article in the *Ladies' Home Journal* with the attractive title, 'Everybody Ought to be Rich'. In it Mr Raskob pointed out that anyone who saved fifteen dollars a month, invested it in sound common stocks, and spent no dividends would be

1. ibid., Pt. III, Chap. 2, p. 39.
2. *Stock Exchange Practices*, Report, Washington, 1934, pp. 103-4.

worth – as it then appeared – some eighty thousand dollars after twenty years. Obviously, at this rate, a great many people could be rich.

But there was the twenty-year delay. Twenty years seemed a long time to get rich, especially in 1929, and for a Democrat and friend of the people to commit himself to such gradualism was to risk being thought a reactionary. Mr Raskob, therefore, had a further suggestion. He proposed an investment trust which would be specifically designed to allow the poor man to increase his capital just as the rich man was doing.

The plan, which Mr Raskob released to the public in the early summer of 1929, was worked out in some detail. (The author stated that he had discussed it with 'financiers, economists, theorists, professors, bankers, labour leaders, industrial leaders, and many men of no prominence who have ideas'.) A company would be organized to buy stocks. The proletarian with, say, $200 would turn over his pittance to the company which would then buy stocks in the rather less meagre amount of $500. The additional $300 the company would get from a financial subsidiary organized for the purpose, and with which it would post all of the stock as collateral. The incipient capitalist would pay off his debt at the rate of perhaps $25 a month. He would, of course, get the full benefit of the increase in the value of the stock, and this was something that Mr Raskob regarded as inevitable. Hammering home the inadequacy of existing arrangements, Mr Raskob said: 'Now all the man with $200 to $500 to invest can do today is to buy Liberty bonds . . .'[1]

The reaction to the Raskob plan was comparable to the response to a new and daring formulation of the relation of mass to energy. 'A practical Utopia', one paper called it. Another described it as 'The greatest vision of Wall Street's greatest mind'. A tired and cynical commentator was moved

1. *The Literary Digest*, 1 June 1929.

to say that it looks 'more like financial statesmanship than anything that has come out of Wall Street in many a weary moon'.[1]

Had there been a little more time, it seems certain that
something would have been made of Mr Raskob's plan.
People were full of enthusiasm for the wisdom and perspicacity
of such men. This was admirably indicated by the willingness
of people to pay for the genius of the professional financier.

## 5

The measure of this respect for financial genius was the relation
of the market value of the outstanding securities of the investment trust to the value of the securities it owned. Normally
the securities of the trust were worth considerably more than
the property it owned. Sometimes they were worth twice as
much. There should be no ambiguity on this point. The only
property of the investment trust was the common and preferred stocks and debentures, mortgages, bonds, and cash that
it owned. (Often it had neither office nor office furniture; the
sponsoring firm ran the investment trust out of its own quarters.) Yet, had these securities all been sold on the market,
the proceeds would invariably have been less, and often much
less, than the current value of the outstanding securities of the
investment company. The latter, obviously, had some claim to
value which went well beyond the assets behind them.

That premium was, in effect, the value an admiring community placed on professional financial knowledge, skill, and
manipulative ability. To value a portfolio of stocks 'at the
market' was to regard it only as inert property. But as the
property of an investment trust it was much more, for the
portfolio was then combined with the precious ingredient of
financial genius. Such special ability could invoke a whole
strategy for increasing the value of securities. It could join in

1. ibid.

pools and syndicates to put up values. It knew when others were doing likewise and could go along. Above all, the financial genius was in on things. It had access to what Mr Lawrence of Princeton described as 'the stage whereon is focused the world's most intelligent and best informed judgement of the values of the enterprises which serve men's needs'.[1] One might make money investing directly in Radio, J. I. Case, or Montgomery Ward, but how much safer and wiser to let it be accomplished by the men of peculiar knowledge, and wisdom.

By 1929 the investment trusts were aware of their reputation for omniscience, as well as its importance, and they lost no opportunity to enlarge it. To have a private economist was one possibility, and as the months passed a considerable competition developed for those men of adequate reputation and susceptibility. It was a golden age for professors. The American Founders Group, an awe-inspiring family of investment trusts, had as a director Professor Edwin W. Kemmerer, the famous Princeton money expert. The staff economist was Dr Rufus Tucker, also a well-known figure. (That economists were not yet functioning with perfect foresight is perhaps suggested by the subsequent history of the enterprise. United Founders, the largest company in the group, suffered a net contraction in its assets of $301,385,504 by the end of 1935, and its stock dropped from a high of over $75 share in 1929 to a little under 75 cents.)[2]

Still another great combine was advised by Dr David Friday, who had come to Wall Street from the University of Michigan. Friday's reputation for both insight and foresight was breathtaking. A Michigan trust had three college professors – Irving Fisher of Yale, Joseph S. Davis of Stanford, and Edmund E. Day then of Michigan – to advise on its

1. *Wall Street and Washington*, p. 163.
2. Bernard J. Reis, *False Security*, New York (Equinox), 1937, pp. 117 ff. and 296.

policies.[1] The company stressed not only the diversity of its portfolio but also of its counsel. It was fully protected from any parochial Yale, Stanford, or Michigan view of the market.

Other trusts urged the excellence of their genius in other terms. Thus one observed that, since it owned stocks in 120 corporations, it benefited from the 'combined efficiency of their presidents, officers, and the boards of directors'. It noted further that 'closely allied to these corporations are the great banking institutions'. Then, in something of a logical broad jump, it concluded, 'The trust, therefore, mobilizes to a large extent the successful business intellect of the country.' Another concern, less skilled in logical method, contented itself with pointing out that 'Investing is a science instead of a "one-man job".'[2]

As 1929 wore along, it was plain that more and more of the new investors in the market were relying on the intellect and the science of the trusts. This meant, of course, that they still had the formidable problem of deciding between the good and the bad trusts. That there were some bad ones was (though barely) recognized. Writing in the March 1929 issue of *The Atlantic Monthly*, Paul C. Cabot stated that dishonesty, inattention, inability, and greed were among the common shortcomings of the new industry. These were impressive disadvantages, and as an organizer and officer of a promising investment trust, The State Street Investment Corporation, Mr Cabot presumably spoke with some authority.[3] However, audience response to such warnings in 1929 was very poor. And the warnings were very infrequent.

1. *Investment Trusts and Investment Companies*, Pt I, p. 111.
2. ibid., Pt I, pp. 61, 62.
3. ibid., Pt III, Ch. 1, p. 53.

6

Knowledge, manipulative skill, or financial genius was not the only magic of the investment trust. There was also leverage. By the summer of 1929, one no longer spoke of investment trusts as such. One referred to high-leverage trusts, low-leverage trusts, or trusts without any leverage at all.

The principle of leverage is the same for an investment trust as in the game of crack-the-whip. By the application of well-known physical laws, a modest movement near the point of origin is translated into a major jolt on the extreme periphery. In an investment trust, leverage was achieved by issuing bonds, preferred stock, as well as common stock to purchase, more or less exclusively, a portfolio of common stocks. When the common stock so purchased rose in value, a tendency which was always assumed, the value of the bonds and preferred stock of the trust was largely unaffected.[1] These securities had a fixed value derived from a specified return. Most or all of the gain from rising portfolio values was concentrated on the common stock of the investment trust which, as a result, rose marvellously.

Consider, by way of illustration, the case of an investment trust organized in early 1920 with a capital of $150 million – a plausible size by then. Let it be assumed, further, that a third of the capital was realized from the sale of bonds, a third from preferred stock, and the rest from the sale of common stock. If this $150 million were invested, and if the securities so purchased showed a normal appreciation, the portfolio value would have increased by midsummer by about fifty per cent. The assets would be worth $225 million. The bonds and preferred stock would still be worth only $100 million; their

1. Assuming they were reasonably orthodox. Bonds and preferred stock, in these days, were issues with an almost infinite variety of conversion and participation rights.

earnings would not have increased, and they could claim no greater share of the assets in the hypothetical event of a liquidation of the company. The remaining $125 million, therefore, would underlie the value of the common stock of the trust. The latter, in other words, would have increased in asset value from $50 million to $125 million, or by a hundred and fifty per cent, and as the result of an increase of only fifty per cent in the value of the assets of the trust as a whole.

This was the magic of leverage, but this was not all of it. Were the common stock of the trust, which had so miraculously increased in value, held by still another trust with similar leverage, the common stock of *that* trust would get an increase of between seven hundred and eight hundred per cent from the original fifty per cent advance. And so forth. In 1929 the discovery of the wonders of the geometric series struck Wall Street with a force comparable to the invention of the wheel. There was a rush to sponsor investment trusts which would sponsor investment trusts, which would, in turn, sponsor investment trusts. The miracle of leverage, moreover, made this a relatively costless operation to the ultimate man behind all of the trusts. Having launched one trust and retained a share of the common stock, the capital gains from leverage made it relatively easy to swing a second and larger one which enhanced the gains and made possible a third and still bigger trust.

Thus, Harrison Williams, one of the more ardent exponents of leverage, was thought by the Securities and Exchange Commission to have substantial influence over a combined investment trust and holding company system with a market value in 1929 at close to a billion dollars.[1] This had been built

1. Part of it shared with Goldman, Sachs, as will be noted presently. The line between a holding company, which has investment in and control of an operating company (or another holding company), and

on his original control of a smallish concern – the Central States Electric Corporation – which was worth only some six million dollars in 1921.[1] Leverage was also a prime factor in the remarkable growth of the American Founders Group. The original member of this notable family of investment trusts was launched in 1921. The original promoter was, unhappily, unable to get the enterprise off the ground becaue he was in bankruptcy. However, the following year a friend contributed $500, with which modest capital a second trust was launched, and the two companies began business. The public reception was highly favourable, and by 1927 the two original companies and a third which had subsequently been added had sold between seventy and eighty million dollars' worth of securities to the public.[2] But this was only the beginning; in 1928 and 1929 an explosion of activity struck the Founders Group. Stock was sold to the public at a furious rate. New firms with new names were organized to sell still more stock until, by the end of 1929, there were thirteen companies in the group.

At that time the largest company, the United Founders Corporation, had total resources of $686,165,000. The group as a whole had resources with a market value of more than a billion dollars, which may well have been the largest volume of assets ever controlled by an original outlay of $500. Of the billion dollars, some $320,000,000 was represented by the inter-company holdings – the investment of one or another company of the group in the securities of yet others. This fiscal incest was the instrument through which control was maintained and

an investment trust or company, which has investment but which is presumed not to have control, is often a shadowy one. The pyramiding of holding companies and concomitant leverage effects was also a striking feature of the period.

---

1. *Investment Trusts and Investment Companies*, Pt. III, Ch. 1, pp. 5, 6.

2. ibid., Pt. I, pp. 98–100.

leverage enjoyed. Thanks to this long chain of holdings by one company in another, the increases in values in 1928 and 1929 were effectively concentrated in the value of the common stock of the original companies.

Leverage, it was later to develop, works both ways. Not all of the securities held by the Founders were of a kind calculated to rise indefinitely, much less to resist depression. Some years later the portfolio was found to have contained 5,000 shares of Kreuger and Toll, 20,000 shares of Kolo Products Corporation, an adventuresome new company which was to make soap out of banana oil, and $295,000 in the bonds of the Kingdom of Yugoslavia.[1] As Kreuger and Toll moved down to its ultimate value of nothing, leverage was also at work – geometric series are equally dramatic in reverse. But this aspect of the mathematics of leverage was still unrevealed in early 1929, and notice must first be taken of the most dramatic of all the investment company promotions of that remarkable year, those of Goldman, Sachs.

### 7

Goldman, Sachs and Company, an investment banking and brokerage partnership, came rather late to the investment trust business. Not until 4 December 1928, less than a year before the stock market crash, did it sponsor the Goldman Sachs Trading Corporation, its initial venture in the field. However, rarely, if ever, in history has an enterprise grown as the Goldman Sachs Trading Corporation and its offspring grew in the months ahead.

The initial issue of stock in the Trading Corporation was a million shares, all of which was bought by Goldman, Sachs and Company at $100 a share for a total of $100,000,000. Ninety per cent was then sold to the public at $104. There were no bonds and no preferred stocks; leverage had not yet

1. Reis, op. cit., p. 124.

been discovered by Goldman, Sachs and Company. Control of the Goldman Sachs Trading Corporation remained with Goldman, Sachs and Company by virtue of a management contract and the presence of the partners of the company on the board of the Trading Corporation.[1]

In the two months after its formation, the new company sold some more stock to the public, and on 21 February it merged with another investment trust, the Financial and Industrial Securities Corporation. The assets of the resulting company were valued at $235 million, reflecting a gain of well over a hundred per cent in under three months. By 2 February, roughly three weeks before the merger, the stock for which the original investors had paid $104 was selling for $136.50. Five days later, on 7 February, it reached $222.50. At this latter figure it had a value approximately twice that of the current total worth of the securities, cash, and other assets owned by the Trading Corporation.

This remarkable premium was not the undiluted result of public enthusiasm for the financial genius of Goldman, Sachs. Goldman, Sachs had considerable enthusiasm for itself, and the Trading Corporation was buying heavily of its own securities. By 14 March it had bought 560,724 shares of its own stock for a total outlay of $57,021,936.[2] This, in turn, had boomed their value. However, perhaps foreseeing the exiguous character of an investment company which had its investments all in its own common stock, the Trading Corporation stopped buying itself in March. Then it resold part of the stock to William Crapo Durant, who re-resold it to the public as opportunity allowed.

The spring and early summer were relatively quiet for

1. *Stock Exchange Practices*, Hearings, April–June 1932, Pt 2, pp. 566, 567.

2. Details here are from *Investment Trusts and Investment Companies*, Pt III, Ch. 1, pp. 6 ff. and 17 ff.

Goldman, Sachs, but it was a period of preparation. By 26 July it was ready. On that date the Trading Corporation, jointly with Harrison Williams, launched the Shenandoah Corporation, the first of two remarkable trusts. The initial securities issue by Shenandoah was $102,500,000 (there was an additional issue a couple of months later) and it was reported to have been oversubscribed some sevenfold. There were both preferred and common stock, for by now Goldman, Sachs knew the advantages of leverage. Of the five million shares of common stock in the initial offering, two million were taken by the Trading Corporation, and two million by Central States Electric Corporation on behalf of the co-sponsor, Harrison Williams. Williams was a member of the small board along with partners in Goldman, Sachs. Another board member was a prominent New York attorney whose lack of discrimination in this instance may perhaps be attributed to youthful optimism. It was Mr John Foster Dulles. The stock of Shenandoah was issued at $17.50. There was brisk trading on a 'when issued' basis. It opened at 30, reached a high of 36 and closed at 36, or 18.5 above the issue price. (By the end of the year the price was 8 and a fraction. It later touched fifty cents.)

Meanwhile Goldman, Sachs was already preparing its second tribute to the countryside of Thomas Jefferson, the prophet of small and simple enterprises. This was the even mightier Blue Ridge Corporation, which made its appearance on 20 August. Blue Ridge had a capital of $142,000,000, and nothing about it was more remarkable than the fact that it was sponsored by Shenandoah, its precursor by precisely twenty-five days. Blue Ridge had the same board of directors as Shenandoah, including the still optimistic Mr Dulles, and of its 7,250,000 shares of common stock (there was also a substantial issue of preferred) Shenandoah subscribed a total of 6,250,000. Goldman, Sachs by now was applying leverage with a vengeance.

An interesting feature of Blue Ridge was the opportunity it offered the investor to divest himself of routine securities in direct exchange for the preferred and common stock of the new corporation. A holder of American Telephone and Telegraph Company could receive $4\frac{70}{715}$ shares each of Blue Ridge Preference and Common for each share of Telephone stock turned in. The same privilege was extended to holders of Allied Chemical and Dye, Santa Fe, Eastman Kodak, General Electric, Standard Oil of New Jersey, and some fifteen other stocks. There was much interest in this offer.

20 August, the birthday of Blue Ridge, was a Tuesday, but there was more work to be done by Goldman, Sachs that week. On Thursday, the Goldman Sachs Trading Corporation announced the acquisition of the Pacific American Associates, a West Coast investment trust which, in turn, had recently bought a number of smaller investment trusts and which owned the American Trust Company, a large commercial bank with numerous branches throughout California. Pacific American had a capital of around a hundred million. In preparation for the merger, the Trading Corporation had issued another $71,400,000 in stock which it had exchanged for capital stock of the American Company, the holding company which owned over ninety-nine per cent of the common stock of the American Trust Company.[1]

Having issued more than a quarter of a billion dollars' worth of securities in less than a month – an operation that would not then have been unimpressive for the United States Treasury – activity at Goldman, Sachs subsided somewhat. Its members had not been the only busy people during this time. It was a poor day in August and September of that year when no new trust was announced or no large new issue of securities was

1. Details on Shenandoah, Blue Ridge, and the Pacific American merger not from the *New York Times* of the period are from *Investment Trusts and Investment Companies*, Pt III, Ch. 1, pp. 5–7.

offered by an old one. Thus, on 1 August the papers announced the formation of Anglo-American Shares, Inc., a company which, with a *soigné* touch not often seen in a Delaware corporation, had among its directors the Marquess of Carisbrooke, G.C.B., G.C.V.O., and Colonel the Master of Sempill, A.F.C., otherwise identified as the President of the Royal Aeronautical Society, London. American Insuranstocks Corporation was launched the same day, though boasting no more glamorous a director than William Gibbs McAdoo. On succeeding days came Gude Winmill Trading Corporation, National Republic Investment Trust, Insull Utility Investments, Inc., International Carriers, Ltd, Tri-Continental Allied Corporation, and Solvay American Investment Corporation. On 13 August the papers also announced that an Assistant U.S. Attorney had visited the offices of the Cosmopolitan Fiscal Corporation and also an investment service called the Financial Counsellor. In both cases the principals were absent. The offices of the Financial Counsellor were equipped with a peephole like a speakeasy.

More investment trust securities were offered in September of 1929 even than in August – the total was above $600 million[1]. However, the nearly simultaneous promotion of Shenandoah and Blue Ridge was to stand as the pinnacle of new era finance. It is difficult not to marvel at the imagination which was implicit in this gargantuan insanity. If there must be madness something may be said for having it on a heroic scale.

Years later, on a grey dawn in Washington, the following colloquy occurred before a committee of the United States Senate.[2]

1. E. H. H. Simmons. *The Principal Causes of the Stock Market Crisis of Nineteen Twenty-Nine* (address issued in pamphlet form). New York Stock Exchange, January 1930, p. 16.

2. *Stock Exchange Practices*, Hearings, April–June 1932, Pt 2, pp. 566–7.

SENATOR COUZENS: Did Goldman, Sachs and Company organize the Goldman Sachs Trading Corporation?

MR SACHS: Yes, sir.

SENATOR COUZENS: And it sold its stock to the public?

MR SACHS: A portion of it. The firms invested originally in ten per cent of the entire issue for the sum of $10,000,000.

SENATOR COUZENS: And the other ninety per cent was sold to the public?

MR SACHS: Yes, sir.

SENATOR COUZENS: At what price?

MR SACHS: At 104. That is the old stock . . . the stock was split two for one.

SENATOR COUZENS: And what is the price of the stock now?

MR SACHS: Approximately $1\frac{3}{4}$.

# CHAPTER V

# THE TWILIGHT OF ILLUSION

## I

THERE was no summer lull in Wall Street that year. Along with the great investment trust promotions went the greatest market ever. Every day prices rose; they almost never fell. During June the *Times* industrials went up 52 points; in July they gained another 25. This was a total gain of 77 points in two months. In all of the remarkable year of 1928 they had gone up only 86·5 points. Then in August they rose another 33 points. This gain of 110 points in three months – from 339 on the last day of May to 449 on the last day of August – meant that during the summer values had increased, over-all, by nearly a quarter.

Individual issues had also done very well. During the three summer months, Westinghouse went from 151 to 286 for a net gain of 135. General Electric was up from 268 to 391, and Steel from 165 to 258. Even so sombre a security as American Tel and Tel had gone from 209 to 303. The investment trusts were making good gains. United Founders went from 36 bid to 68; Alleghany Corporation rose from 33 to 56.

The volume of trading was also consistently heavy. On the New York Stock Exchange it was frequently between four and five million shares. Only occasionally on a full day did it drop below three million. However, trading on the New York Stock Exchange was no longer a good index of the total interest in securities speculation. Many new and exciting issues – Shenandoah, Blue Ridge, Pennroad, Insull Utilities – were not listed on the Big Board. The New York Stock Exchange in those days was not a snobbish, prying, or an intolerant

institution. Most companies that so desired could have their
stocks listed. Nevertheless, there were some who found it wise,
and many more who found it convenient not to answer the
fairly elementary requests which were made by the Exchange for
information. The new stocks, accordingly, were traded on the
Curb, or in Boston, or on other out-of-town exchanges.
Although business on the New York Stock Exchange remained larger than that on all other markets combined, its
relative position suffered. (In 1929 it had an estimated sixty-
one per cent of all transactions; three years later, when most
of the new trusts had disappeared forever, the Exchange had
seventy-six per cent of the total business.[1]) It follows that by
the summer of 1929 the normally somnambulant markets of
Boston, San Francisco, and even of Cincinnati were having
a boom. Instead of being merely a pale reflection of the real
thing on Wall Street, they had a life and personality of their
own. Stocks were for sale here that couldn't be had in New
York, and some of them had an exceptional speculative kick.
By 1929 it was a poor town, sadly devoid of civic spirit, which
wasn't wondering if it too shouldn't have a stock market.

More than the prices of common stocks were rising. So, at an
appalling rate, was the volume of speculation. Brokers' loans
during the summer increased at a rate of about $400,000,000
a month. By the end of the summer, the total exceeded seven
billions. Of that more than half was being supplied by corporations and individuals, at home and abroad, who were taking
advantage of the excellent rate of return which New York was
providing on money. Only rarely did the rate on call loans
during that summer get as low as six per cent. The normal
range was seven to twelve. On one ocasion the rate touched
fifteen. Since, as earlier observed, these loans provided all but
total safety, liquidity, and ease of administration, the interest

1. Estimates are from *Stock Exchange Practices*, Report, Washington, 1934, p. 8.

would not have seemed unattractive to a usurious moneylender in Bombay. To a few alarmed observers it seemed as though Wall Street were by way of devouring all the money of the entire world. However, in accordance with the cultural practice, as the summer passed, the sound and responsible spokesmen decried not the increase in brokers' loans, but those who insisted on attaching significance to this trend. There was a sharp criticism of the prophets of doom.

2

There were two sources of intelligence on brokers' loans. One was the monthly tabulation of the New York Stock Exchange, which in general is used here. The other was the slightly less complete return of the Federal Reserve System which was published weekly. Each Friday this report showed a large increase in loans; each Friday it was firmly stated that it didn't mean a thing, and anyone who suggested otherwise was administered a stern rebuke. It seems probable that only a minority of the people in the market related the volume of the brokers' loans to the volume of purchases on margin and thence to the amount of speculation. Accordingly, an expression of concern over these loans was easily attacked as a gratuitous effort to undermine confidence. Thus, in *Barron's* on 8 July, Sheldon Sinclair Wells explained that those who worried about brokers' loans, and about the influx of funds from corporations, simply did not know what was going on. The call market had become a great new investment outlet for corporate reserves, he argued. The critics did not appreciate this change.

Chairman Mitchell of the National City Bank, by nature an equable man, was repeatedly angered by the attention being given to brokers' loans and expressed himself strongly. The financial press was also disturbed, and when Arthur Brisbane later in the year questioned the propriety of a ten per cent call rate, *The Wall Street Journal* reached the end of its patience. 'Even in general newspapers some accurate knowledge is required for discussing most things. Why is it that any ignoramus can talk about Wall Street?'[1] (It does seem possible that Brisbane thought the rate was ten per cent a day rather than a year.)

Scholars also reacted against those who, deliberately or otherwise, were sabotaging prosperity with their unguarded pessimism. After soberly viewing the situation, Professor Dice concluded that the high level of brokers' loans should not be 'as greatly feared as some would have us believe'[2]. In August the Midland Bank of Cleveland made public the results of calculations which proved that until loans by corporations in the stock market reached twelve billion there was no cause for concern.[3]

The best reassurance on brokers' loans was in the outlook for the market. If stocks remained high and went higher, and if they did so because their prospects justified their price, then there was no occasion to worry about the loans that were piling up. Accordingly, much of the defence of the loans consisted in defending the levels of the market. It was not hard to persuade people that the market was sound; as always in such times they asked only that the disturbing voices of doubt be muted and that there be tolerably frequent expressions of confidence.

In 1929 treason had not yet become a casual term of reproach. As a result, pessimism was not openly equated with efforts to destroy the American way of life. Yet it had such connotations. Almost without exception, those who expressed concern said subsequently that they did so with fear and trepidation. (Later in the year a Boston firm of investment counsellors struck a modern note with a widely publicized warning that America had no place for 'destructionists'.)

1. *The Wall Street Journal*, 19 September 1929.
2. *New Levels in the Stock Market*, p. 183.
3. *New York Times*, 2 August 1929.

The official optimists were many and articulate. Thus in June, Bernard Baruch told Bruce Barton, in a famous interview published in *The American Magazine*,[1] that the 'economic condition of the world seems on the verge of a great forward movement'. He pointed out that no bears had houses on Fifth Avenue. Numerous college professors also exuded scientific confidence. In light of later developments, the record of the Ivy League was especially unfortunate. In a statement which achieved minor notoriety, Lawrence of Princeton said that 'the consensus of judgement of the millions whose valuations function on that admirable market, the Stock Exchange, is that stocks are not at present over-valued'. He added: 'Where is that group of men with the all-embracing wisdom which will entitle them to veto the judgement of this intelligent multitude?'[2]

That autumn Professor Irving Fisher of Yale made his immortal estimate: 'Stock prices have reached what looks like a permanently high plateau.' Irving Fisher was the most original of American economists. Happily there are better things – his contributions to index numbers, technical economic theory, and monetary theory – for which he is remembered.

From Cambridge slightly less spacious reassurance came from the Harvard Economic Society, an extracurricular enterprise conducted by a number of economics professors of unexceptional conservatism. The purpose of the Society was to help businessmen and speculators foretell the future. Forecasts were made several times a month and undoubtedly gained in stature from their association with the august name of the university.

By wisdom or good luck, the Society in early 1929 was

1. *The American Magazine*, June 1929.
2. *Wall Street and Washington*, p. 179. These passages were later quoted editorially by the *New York Times* and are reproduced in turn from there.

mildly bearish. Its forecasters had happened to decide that a recession (though assuredly not a depression) was overdue. Week by week they foretold a slight setback in business. When, by the summer of 1929, the setback had not appeared, at least in any very visible form, the Society gave up and confessed error. Business, it decided, might be good after all. This, as such things are judged, was still a creditable record, but then came the crash. The Society remained persuaded that no serious depression was in prospect. In November it said firmly that 'a severe depression like that of 1920–21 is outside the range of probability. We are not facing protracted liquidation.' This view the Society reiterated until it was liquidated.

## 3

The bankers were also a source of encouragement to those who wished to believe in the permanence of the boom. A great many of them abandoned their historic role as the guardians of the nation's fiscal pessimism and enjoyed a brief respite of optimism. They had reasons for doing so. In the years preceding, a considerable number of the commercial banks, including the largest of the New York houses, had organized securities affiliates. These affiliates sold stocks and bonds to the public, and this business had become important. It was a business that compelled a rosy view of the future. In addition, individual bankers, perhaps taking a cue from the heads of the National City and Chase in New York, were speculating vigorously on their own behalf. They were unlikely to say, much less advocate, anything that would jar the market.

However, there were exceptions. One was Paul M. Warburg of the International Acceptance Bank, whose predictions must be accorded the same prominence as the forecasts of Irving Fisher. They were remarkably prescient. In March 1929, he called for a stronger Federal Reserve policy and argued that if the present orgy of 'unrestrained speculation' were not brought promptly to a halt there would ultimately be a disastrous collapse. This, he suggested, would be unfortunate not alone for the speculators. It would 'bring about a general depression involving the entire country'.[1]

Only Wall Street spokesmen who took the most charitable view of Warburg contented themselves with describing him as obsolete. One said he was 'sandbagging American prosperity'. Others hinted that he had a motive – presumably a short position. As the market went up and up, his warnings were recalled only with contempt.[2]

The most notable sceptics were provided by the press. They were a great minority to be sure. Most magazines and most newspapers in 1929 reported the upward sweep of the market with admiration and awe and without alarm. They viewed both the present and the future with exuberance. Moreover, by 1929 numerous journalists were sternly resisting the more subtle blandishments and flattery to which they have been thought susceptible. Instead they were demanding cold cash for news favourable to the market. A financial columnist of the *Daily News*, who signed himself 'The Trader', received some $19,000 in 1929 and early 1930 from a free-lance operator named John J. Levenson. 'The Trader' repeatedly spoke well of stocks in which Mr Levenson was interested. Mr Levenson later insisted, however, that this was a coincidence and the payment reflected his more or less habitual generosity.[3] A radio commentator named William J. McMahon was the president of the McMahon Institute of Economic Research, an organization that was mostly McMahon. He told in his

1. *The Commercial and Financial Chronicle*, 9 March 1929, p. 1444.
2. Alexander Dana Noyes, *The Market Place*, Boston (Little, Brown), 1938, p. 324.
3. *Stock Exchange Practices*, Hearings, April–June 1932, Pt 2, pp. 601 ff.

broadcasts of the brilliant prospects of stocks which pool operators were seeking to boom. For this, it later developed, he received an honorarium of $250 a week from a certain David M. Lion.[1] Mr Lion was one of several whom the Pecora Committee reported as making a business of buying favourable comment in the necessary amount at the proper moment.

At the other extreme was the best of the financial press. The established financial services like Poor's and that of the Standard Statistics Company never lost touch with reality. In the autumn Poor's *Weekly Business and Investment Letter* went so far as to speak of the 'great common-stock delusion'.[2] The editor of *The Commercial and Financial Chronicle* was never quite shaken in his conviction that Wall Street had taken leave of its senses. The weekly reports on the brokers' loans were regularly the occasion for a solemn warning; the news columns featured any available bad news. However, by far the greatest force for sobriety was the *New York Times*. Under the guidance of the veteran Alexander Dana Noyes, its financial page was all but immune to the blandishments of the New Era. A regular reader could not doubt that a day of reckoning was expected. Also, on several occasions it reported, much too prematurely, that the day of reckoning had arrived.

Indeed the temporary breaks in the market which preceded the crash were a serious trial for those who had declined fantasy. Early in 1928, in June, in December, and in February and March of 1929 it seemed that the end had come. On various of these occasions the *Times* happily reported the return to reality. And then the market took flight again. Only a durable sense of doom could survive such discouragement. The time was coming when the optimists would reap a rich harvest of discredit. But it has long since been forgotten that for many

1. *Stock Exchange Practices*, Hearings, April–June 1932, Pt 2, pp. 676 ff.
2. Quoted by Allen, *Only Yesterday*, p. 322.

months those who resisted reassurance were similarly, if less permanently, discredited. To say that the *Times*, when the real crash came, reported the event with jubilation would be an exaggeration. Nevertheless, it covered it with an unmistakable absence of sorrow.

## 4

By the summer of 1929 the market not only dominated the news. It also dominated the culture. That *recherché* minority which at other times has acknowledged its interest in Saint Thomas Aquinas, Proust, psychoanalysis, and psychosomatic medicine then spoke of United Corporation, United Founders, and Steel. Only the most aggressive of the eccentrics maintained their detachment from the market and their interest in auto-suggestion or communism. Main Street had always had one citizen who could speak knowingly about buying or selling stocks. Now he became an oracle. In New York, on the edge of any gathering of significantly interesting people there had long been a literate broker or investment counsellor who was abreast of current plans for pools, syndicates, and mergers, and was aware of attractive possibilities. He helpfully advised his friends on investments, and pressed, he would always tell what he knew of the market and much that he didn't. Now these men, even in the company of artists, playwrights, poets, and beautiful concubines, suddenly shone forth. Their words, more or less literally, became golden. Their audience listened not with the casual heed of people who are collecting quotable epigrams, but with the truly rapt attention of those who expect to make money by what they hear.

That much of what was repeated about the market – then as now – bore no relation to reality is important, but not remarkable. Between human beings there is a type of intercourse which proceeds not from knowledge, or even from lack of knowledge, but from failure to know what isn't known. This was true of much of the discourse on the market. At luncheon in downtown Scranton, the knowledgeable physician spoke of the impending split-up in the stock of Western Utility Investors and the effect on prices. Neither the doctor nor his listeners knew why there should be a split-up, why it should increase values, or even why Western Utility Investors should have any value. But neither the doctor nor his audience knew that he did not know. Wisdom, itself, is often an abstraction associated not with fact or reality but with the man who asserts it and the manner of its assertion.

Perhaps the failure to visualize the extent of one's innocence was especially true of women investors, who by now were entering the market in increasing numbers. (An article in *The North American Review* in April reported that women had become important players of 'man's most exciting capitalistic game' and that the modern housewife now 'reads, for instance, that Wright Aero is going up . . . just as she does that fresh fish is now on the market . . .' The author hazarded the guess that success in speculation would do a lot for women's prestige.) To the typical female plunger the association of Steel was not with a corporation, and certainly not with mines, ships, railroads, blast furnaces, and open hearths. Rather it was with symbols on a tape and lines on a chart and a price that went up. She spoke of Steel with the familiarity of an old friend, when in fact she knew nothing of it whatever. Nor would anyone tell her that she did not know that she did not know. We are a polite and cautious people, and we avoid unpleasantness. Moreover, such advice, so far from accomplishing any result, would only have inspired a feeling of contempt for anyone who lacked the courage and the initiative and the sophistication to see how easily one could become rich. The lady operator had discovered she could be rich. Surely her right to be rich was as good as anyone's.

One of the uses of women is that their motivations, though often similar, are less elaborately disguised than those of men.

The values of a society totally preoccupied with making money are not altogether reassuring. During the summer, the *Times* accepted the copy of a dealer in the securities of the National Waterworks Corporation, a company which had been organized to buy into city water companies. The advertisement carried the following acquisitive thought: 'Picture this scene today, if by some cataclysm only one small well should remain for the great city of New York – $1.00 a bucket, $100, $1,000, $1,000,000. The man who owned the well would own the wealth of the city.' All cataclysmically minded investors were urged to get a long position in water before it was too late.

## 5

The polar role of the stock market in American life in the summer of 1929 is beyond doubt. And many people of many different kinds and conditions were in the stock market. Frederick Lewis Allen pictured the diversity of this participation in a fine passage:

The rich man's chauffeur drove with his ears laid back to catch the news of an impending move in Bethlehem Steel; he held fifty shares himself on a twenty-point margin. The window-cleaner at the broker's office paused to watch the ticker, for he was thinking of converting his laboriously accumulated savings into a few shares of Simmons. Edwin Lefèvre (an articulate reporter on the market at this time who could claim considerable personal experience) told of a broker's valet who made nearly a quarter of a million in the market, of a trained nurse who cleaned up thirty thousand following the tips given her by grateful patients; and of a Wyoming cattleman, thirty miles from the nearest railroad, who bought or sold a thousand shares a day.[1]

Yet there is probably more danger of overestimating rather

1. *Only Yesterday*, p. 315.

than underestimating the popular interest in the market. The cliché that by 1929 everyone 'was in the market' is far from the literal truth. Then, as now, to the great majority of workers, farmers, white-collar workers, indeed to the great majority of all Americans, the stock market was a remote and vaguely ominous thing. Then, as now, not many knew how one went about buying a security; the purchase of stocks on margin was in every respect as remote from life as the casino at Monte Carlo.

In later years, a Senate committee investigating the securities markets undertook to ascertain the number of people who were involved in securities speculation in 1929. The member firms of twenty-nine exchanges in that year reported themselves as having accounts with a total of 1,548,707 customers. (Of these, 1,371,920 were customers of member firms of the New York Stock Exchange.) Thus only one and a half million people, out of a population of approximately 120 million and of between 29 and 30 million families, had an active association of any sort with the stock market. And not all of these were speculators. Brokerage firms estimated for the Senate committee that only about 600,000 of the accounts just mentioned were for margin trading, as compared with roughly 950,000 in which trading was for cash.

The figure of 600,000 for margin traders involves some duplication – a few large operators had accounts with more than one broker. There were also some traders whose operations were insignificant. However, some speculators are included among the 950,000 cash customers. Some were putting up the full purchase price for their securities, although speculating nonetheless. Some were borrowing money outside the market and posting the securities as collateral. Though listed as cash customers, they were in effect buying on margin. However, it is safe to say that at the peak in 1929 the number of active speculators was less – and probably was much less – than a million. Between the end of 1928 and the end of July

1929, a period when the popular folklore has Americans rushing like lemmings to participate in the market, the number of margin accounts on all of the exchanges of the country increased by only slightly more than fifty thousand.[1] The striking thing about the stock market speculation of 1929 was not the massiveness of the participation. Rather it was the way it became central to the culture.

## 6

By the end of the summer of 1929, brokers' bulletins and letters no longer contented themselves with saying what stocks would rise that day and by how much. They went on to say that at 2 p.m. Radio or General Motors would be 'taken in hand'.[2] The conviction that the market had become the personal instrument of mysterious but omnipotent men was never stronger. And, indeed, this was a period of exceedingly active pool and syndicate operations – in short, of manipulation. During 1929 more than a hundred issues on the New York Stock Exchange were subject to manipulative operations, in which members of the Exchange or their partners had participated. The nature of these operations varied somewhat but, in a typical operation, a number of traders pooled their resources to boom a particular stock. They appointed a pool manager, promised not to double-cross each other by private operations, and the pool manager then took a position in the stock which might also include shares contributed by the participants. This buying would increase prices and attract the interest of people watching the tape across the country. The interest of the latter would then be further stimulated by active selling and buying, all of which gave the impression that something big was afloat. Tipsheets and market

1. *Stock Exchange Practices*, Report, 1934, pp. 9, 10.
2. Noyes, op. cit., p. 328.

commentators would tell of exciting developments in the offing. If all went well, the public would come in to buy, and prices would rise on their own. The pool manager would then sell out, pay himself a percentage of the profits, and divide the rest with his investors.[1]

While it lasted, there was never a more agreeable way of making money. The public at large sensed the attractiveness of these operations, and as the summer passed it came to be supposed that Wall Street was concerned with little else. This was an exaggeration, but it did not discourage public activity in the market. People did not believe they were being shorn. Nor were they. Both they and the pool operators were making money with the difference, only, that the latter were making more. In any case, the public reaction to inside operations was to hope that it might get some inside information on these operations and so get a cut in the profits that the great men like Cutten, Livermore, Raskob, and the rest were making.

As the market came to be considered less and less a long-run register of corporate prospects and more and more a product of manipulative artifice, the speculator was required to give it his closest, and preferably his undivided attention. Signs of incipient pool activity had to be detected at the earliest possible moment, which meant that one needed to have his eyes on the tape. However, even the person who was relying on hunches, incantations, or simple faith, as distinct from the effort to assess the intentions of the professionals, found it hard to be out of touch. Only in the case of the rarest individuals can speculation be a part-time activity. Money for most people is far too important. Of the South Sea Bubble it was observed that 'Statesmen forgot their Politics, Lawyers the Bar, Merchants their Traffic, Physicians their Patients, Tradesmen their Shops, Debtors of Quality their Creditors, Divines the Pulpit, and even the Women themselves their Pride and

1. *Stock Exchange Practices*, Report, 1934, pp. 30 ff.

Vanity!'[1] And so it was in 1929. 'Brokers' offices were crowded from 10 a.m. to 3 p.m. with seated or standing customers who, instead of attending to their own business, were watching the blackboard. In some "customers' rooms" it was difficult to get access to a spot from which the posted quotations could be seen; no one could get a chance to inspect the tape.'[2]

It follows that to be out of touch with the market, ever so briefly, was a nerve-racking experience. Happily, this was not often necessary. Ticker service was now nationwide; a local telephone call would get the latest quotations from almost anywhere. A journey to Europe provided one of the few troublesome exceptions. As *The Literary Digest* pointed out during the course of the summer, 'Transoceanic brokerage business has been growing to immense proportions ... But there has been an interlude of uncertainty and inconvenience for speculators crossing the ocean.'[3] In August even this interlude was eliminated. Progressive brokerage houses – a leader was M. J. Meehan, the specialist in Radio and a veteran of many notable manipulations – installed branches on the big ships under special regulations laid down by the Exchange. On 17 August, the *Leviathan* and the *Île de France* left port fully equipped for speculation on the high seas. Business on the *Île* the opening day was described as brisk. One of the first transactions was by Irving Berlin, who sold 1,000 shares of Paramount-Famous-Lasky at 72. (It was a shrewd move. The stock later went more or less to nothing and the company into bankruptcy.)

In Spokane an anonymous poet on the editorial staff of the *Spokesman-Review* celebrated the seagoing boardrooms.

> *We were crowded in the cabin*
> *Watching figures on the Board;*

1. Viscount Erleigh, *The South Sea Bubble*, New York (Putnam), 1933, p. 11.
2. Noyes, op. cit., p. 328.
3. *The Literary Digest*, 31 August 1929.

*It was midnight on the ocean*
*And a tempest loudly roared.*

.    .    .    .

*'We are lost!' the Captain shouted,*
*As he staggered down the stairs.*

*'I've got a tip,' he faltered,*
*'Straight by wireless from the aunt*
*Of a fellow who's related*
*To a cousin of Durant.'*

*At these awful words we shuddered,*
*And the stoutest bull grew sick*
*While the brokers cried, 'More margin!'*
*And the ticker ceased to tick.*

*But the captain's little daughter*
*Said, 'I do not understand –*
*Isn't Morgan on the ocean*
*Just the same as on the land?'*[1]

## 7

Labour Day brought the summer of 1929 to its conventional
end on 2 September. There was a severe heat wave, and on the
evening of the holiday returning motorists tied up the roads
around New York for miles. In the end many were forced to
abandon their vehicles and make their way home by train or
subway. On 3 September the city continued to swelter in what
the Weather Bureau reported was the hottest day of the year.

Away from Wall Street this was a very quiet day in a very
tranquil time. Years later Frederick Lewis Allen went to the
newspapers for that day and in a charming article told all that
he found.[2] There wasn't much. Disarmament was being discussed in that customarily desultory fashion which doubtless

1. Quoted in *The Literary Digest*, 31 August 1929.
2. 'One Day in History', *Harper's Magazine*, November 1937.

in the end will destroy us. The Graf Zeppelin was nearing the end of its first round-the-world flight. A tri-motored plane of Transcontinental Air Transport had crashed in a thunderstorm in New Mexico, and eight were killed. (The line had only recently inaugurated a forty-eight-hour service to the West Coast – railway sleeper to Columbus, Ohio, plane to Waynoka, Oklahoma, sleeper again to Clovis, New Mexico, and a plane the rest of the way.) Babe Ruth had knocked out forty home runs so far in the season. As a best-seller, *All Quiet on the Western Front* held a commanding lead over *Dodsworth*. Women's dresses were all emphasizing a decidedly flat look without anyone's saying so. From Washington it was announced that Harry F. Sinclair, then in the District of Columbia jail for being in contempt of the Senate during the Teapot Dome investigations, would henceforth be more closely confined. Previously he had been going daily by automobile to the office of the jail physician whom he was serving as a 'pharmaceutical assistant'. Earlier in the year Sinclair's stock market operations were on a huge scale, and they were later the subject of detailed investigation. It was never shown whether the Washington sojourn involved any important interruption. It seems most unlikely that it did. Mr Sinclair was one of the most resourceful and resilient entrepreneurs of his generation.

On 3 September sales on the New York Stock Exchange were 4,438,910 shares; call money was nine per cent all day; the rate at the banks on prime commercial paper was six and a half per cent; the rediscount rate at the New York Federal Reserve Bank was six per cent. The market was strong with what the market operators called a good undertone.

American Tel and Tel reached 304 that day. U.S. Steel reached 262; General Electric was 396; J. I. Case, 350; New York Central, 256; Radio Corporation of America, adjusted for earlier split-ups and still not having paid a dividend, was 505. The brokers' loan figures of the Federal Reserve, when they were released, also showed another huge increase – $137,000,000 in one week. The New York banks were also borrowing heavily from the Federal Reserve to carry the speculative superstructure – their borrowings during the week increased by $64,000,000. In August the flow of gold to New York from abroad had continued large. Yet the new month seemed to be opening well. There were several expressions of confidence.

On 3 September, by common consent, the great bull market of the nineteen-twenties came to an end. Economics, as always, vouchsafes us few dramatic turning points. Its events are invariably fuzzy or even indeterminate. On some days that followed – a few only – some averages were actually higher. However, never again did the market manifest its old confidence. The later peaks were not peaks but brief interruptions of a downward trend.

On 4 September, the tone of the market was still good, and then on 5 September came a break. The *Times* industrials dropped 10 points, and many individual stocks much more. The blue chips held up fairly well, although Steel went from 255 to 246, while Westinghouse lost 7 points and Tel and Tel 6. Volume mounted sharply as people sought to unload, and 5,565,280 shares were traded on the New York Stock Exchange.

The immediate cause of the break was clear – and interesting. Speaking before his Annual National Business Conference on 5 September, Roger Babson observed, 'Sooner or later a crash is coming, and it may be terrific.' He suggested that what had happened in Florida would now happen in Wall Street, and with customary precision stated that the (Dow-Jones) market averages would probably drop 60–80 points. In a burst of cheer he concluded that 'factories will shut down ... men will be thrown out of work ... the vicious circle will get in full swing and the result will be a serious business depression'.[1]

This was not exactly reassuring. Yet it was a problem why

1. *The Commercial and Financial Chronicle*, 7 September 1929.

the market suddenly should pay attention to Babson. As many hastened to say, he had made many predictions before, and they had not affected prices much one way or another. Moreover, Babson was not a man who inspired confidence as a prophet in the manner of Irving Fisher or the Harvard Economic Society. As an educator, philosopher, theologian, statistician, forecaster, economist, and friend of the law of gravity, he has sometimes been thought to spread himself too thin. The methods by which he reached his conclusions were a problem. They involved a hocus-pocus of lines and areas on a chart. Intuition, and possibly even mysticism, played a part. Those who employed rational, objective, and scientific methods were naturally uneasy about Babson, although their methods failed to foretell the crash. In these matters, as often in our culture, it is far, far better to be wrong in a respectable way than to be right for the wrong reasons.

Wall Street was not at loss as to what to do about Babson. It promptly and soundly denounced him. *Barron's*, in an editorial on 9 September, referred to him with heavy irony as the 'sage of Wellesley' and said he should not be taken seriously by anyone acquainted with the 'notorious inaccuracy' of his past statements. The Stock Exchange house of Hornblower and Weeks sternly told its customers: 'We would not be stampeded into selling stocks because of a gratuitous forecast of a bad break in the market by a well-known statistician.'[1] Irving Fisher also took issue. He noted that dividends were rising, that the suspicion of common stocks was receding, and that investment trusts now offered the investor 'wide and well-managed diversification'. His own conclusion was: 'There may be a recession in stock prices, but not anything in the nature of a crash.'[2] Developing a slightly different theme, a Boston investment trust told the public that it should be

1. Quoted in *The Wall Street Journal*, 6 September 1929.
2. Edward Angly, *Oh, Yeah!*, New York (Viking), 1931, p. 37.

prepared for slight setbacks, but it should realize that they would soon pass. In large advertisements it pointed out that 'When temporary breaks come, *indentations in the ever-ascending curve of American prosperity*, individual stocks, even of the most successful companies, go down with the general list . . .' However, it also stated on its own behalf that 'Incorporated Investors lands on a cushion'.

The Babson Break, as it was promptly called, came on a Thursday. The market rallied on Friday and was firm on Saturday. People seemed to be over their fear. It looked as though the ever-ascending curve would start up again, as so often before and Mr Babson notwithstanding. Then on the following week – the week of 9 September – prices were again ragged. On Monday, the *Times*, with the caution born of much premature pessimism, hinted that the end had come and added, 'It is a well-known characteristic of "boom times" that the idea of their being terminated in the old, unpleasant way is rarely recognized as possible.' On Wednesday, in a fine example of market prose, *The Wall Street Journal* observed that 'price movements in the main body of stocks yesterday continued to display the characteristics of a major advance temporarily halted for technical readjustment'.

The unevenness continued. On some days the market was strong; on others it was weak. The direction was slightly, erratically, but, viewed in retrospect, quite definitely down. New investment trusts were still being formed; more speculators were flocking to the market, and the volume of brokers' loans continued sharply up. The end had come, but it was not yet in sight.

Perhaps this was as well. The last moments of life should be cherished, as Wall Street had been told. On 11 September, in keeping with a regular practice, *The Wall Street Journal* printed its thought for the day. It was from Mark Twain:

Don't part with your illusions; when they are gone you may still exist, but you have ceased to live.

# CHAPTER VI

# THE CRASH

I

ACCORDING to the accepted view of events, by the autumn of 1929 the economy was well into a depression. In June the indexes of industrial and of factory production both reached a peak and turned down. By October, the Federal Reserve index of industrial production stood at 117 as compared with 126 four months earlier. Steel production declined from June on; in October freight-car loadings fell. Home-building, a most mercurial industry, had been falling for several years, and it slumped still further in 1929. Finally, down came the stock market. A penetrating student of the economic behaviour of this period has said that the market slump 'reflected, in the main, the change which was already apparent in the industrial situation'.[1]

Thus viewed, the stock market is but a mirror which, perhaps as in this instance, somewhat belated, provides an image of the underlying or *fundamental* economic situation. Cause and effect run from the economy to the stock market, never the reverse. In 1929 the economy was headed for trouble. Eventually that trouble was violently reflected in Wall Street.

In 1929 there were good, or at least strategic, reasons for this view, and it is easy to understand why it has become high doctrine. In Wall Street, as elsewhere in 1929, few people wanted a bad depression. In Wall Street, as elsewhere, there is deep faith in the power of incantation. When the market fell many Wall Street citizens immediately sensed the real danger, which was that income and employment – prosperity in general

1. Thomas Wilson, *Fluctuations in Income and Employment*, p. 143.

– would be adversely affected. This had to be prevented. Preventive incantation required that as many important people as possible repeat as firmly as they could that it wouldn't happen. This they did. They explained how the stock market was merely the froth and that the real substance of economic life rested in production, employment, and spending, all of which would remain unaffected. No one knew for sure that this was so. As an instrument of economic policy, incantation does not permit of minor doubts or scruples.

In the later years of depression it was important to continue emphasizing the unimportance of the stock market. The depression was an exceptionally disagreeable experience. Wall Street has not always been a cherished symbol in our national life. In some of the devout regions of the nation, those who speculate in stocks – the even more opprobrious term gamblers is used – are not counted the greatest moral adornments of our society. Any explanation of the depression which attributed importance to the market collapse would accordingly have been taken very seriously, and it would have meant serious trouble for Wall Street. Wall Street, no doubt, would have survived, but there would have been scars. We should be clear that no deliberate conspiracy existed to minimize the consequences of the Wall Street crash for the economy. Rather, it merely appeared to everyone with an instinct for conservative survival that Wall Street had better be kept out of it. It was vulnerable.

In fact, any satisfactory explanation of the events of the autumn of 1929 and thereafter must accord a dignified role to the speculative boom and ensuing collapse. Until September or October of 1929 the decline in economic activity was very modest. As I shall argue later, until the market crash one could reasonably assume that this downward movement might soon reverse itself, as a similar movement had reversed itself in 1927 or did subsequently in 1949. There were no reasons for expecting disaster. No one could foresee that production, prices, incomes, and all other indicators would continue to shrink through three long and dismal years. Only after the market crash were there plausible grounds to suppose that things might now for a long while get a lot worse.

From the foregoing it follows that the crash did not come – as some have suggested – because the market suddenly became aware that a serious depression was in the offing. A depression, serious or otherwise, could not be foreseen when the market fell. There is still the possibility that the downturn in the indexes frightened the speculators, led them to unload their stocks, and so punctured a bubble that had in any case to be punctured one day. This is more plausible. Some people who were watching the indexes may have been persuaded by this intelligence to sell, and others may then have been encouraged to follow. This is not very important, for it is in the nature of a speculative boom that almost anything can collapse it. Any serious shock to confidence can cause sales by those speculators who have always hoped to get out before the final collapse, but after all possible gains from rising prices have been reaped. Their pessimism will infect those simpler souls who had thought the market might go up forever but who will now change their minds and sell. Soon there will be margin calls, and still others will be forced to sell. So the bubble breaks.

Along with the downturn of the indexes Wall Street has always attributed importance to two other events in the pricking of the bubble. In England on 20 September 1929 the enterprises of Clarence Hatry suddenly collapsed. Hatry was one of those curiously un-English figures with whom the English periodically find themselves unable to cope. Although his earlier financial history had been anything but reassuring, Hatry in the twenties had built up an industrial and financial empire of truly impressive proportions. The nucleus, all the more remarkably, was a line of coin-in-the-slot vending and automatic photograph machines. From these unprepossessing enterprises he had marched on into investment trusts and high finance. His expansion owed much to the issuance of un-authorized stock, the increase of assets by the forging of stock certificates, and other equally informal financing. In the lore of 1929, the unmasking of Hatry in London is supposed to have struck a sharp blow to confidence in New York.[1]

Ranking with Hatry in this lore was the refusal on 11 October of the Massachusetts Department of Public Utilities to allow Boston Edison to split its stocks four to one. As the company argued, such split-ups were much in fashion. To avoid going along was to risk being considered back in the corporate gas-light era. The refusal was unprecedented. Moreover, the Department added insult to injury by announcing an investigation of the company's rates and by suggesting that the present value of the stock, 'due to the action of speculators', had reached a level where 'no one, in our judgement ... on the basis of its earnings, would find it to his advantage to buy it'.

These were uncouth words. They could have been important as, conceivably, could have been the exposure of Clarence Hatry. But it could also be that the inherently unstable equilibrium was shattered simply by a spontaneous decision to get out. On 22 September, the financial pages of the New York papers carried an advertisement of an investment service with the arresting headline, OVERSTAYING A BULL MARKET. Its message read as follows: 'Most investors make money in a bull market, only to lose all profits made – and sometimes more – in the readjustment that inevitably follows.' Instead of the down-turn in the Federal Reserve industrial index, the exposure of Hatry, or the unnatural obstinacy of the Massachusetts Department of Public Utilities, it could have been such thoughts stirring first in dozens and then in hundreds and finally in thousands of breasts which finally brought an end to

1. Hatry pleaded guilty and early in 1930 was given a long jail sentence.

the boom. What first stirred these doubts we do not know, but neither is it very important that we know.

2

Confidence did not disintegrate at once. As noted, through September and into October, although the trend of the market was generally down, good days came with the bad. Volume was high. On the New York Stock Exchange sales were nearly always above four million, and frequently above five. In September new issues appeared in even greater volume than in August, and they regularly commanded a premium over the offering price. On 20 September the *Times* noted that the stock of the recently launched Lehman Corporation which had been offered at $104 had sold the day before at $136. (In the case of this well-managed investment trust the public enthusiasm was not entirely misguided.) During September brokers' loans increased by nearly $670 million, by far the largest increase of any month to date. This showed that speculative zeal had not diminished.

Other signs indicated that the gods of the New Era were still in their temples. In its 12 October issue, *The Saturday Evening Post* had a lead story by Isaac F. Marcosson on Ivar Kreuger. This was a scoop, for Kreuger had previously been inaccessible to journalists. 'Kreuger,' Marcosson observed, 'like Hoover, is an engineer. He has consistently applied engineer precision to the welding of his far-flung industry.' And this was not the only resemblance. 'Like Hoover,' the author added, 'Kreuger rules through pure reason.'

In the interview Kreuger was remarkably candid on one point. He told Mr Marcosson: 'Whatever success I have had may perhaps be attributable to three things: one is silence, the second is more silence, while the third is still more silence.' This was so. Two and a half years later Kreuger committed suicide in his Paris apartment, and shortly thereafter it was discovered that his aversion to divulging information, especially if accurate, had kept even his most intimate acquaintances in ignorance of the greatest fraud in history. His American underwriters, the eminently respectable firm of Lee, Higginson and Company of Boston, had heard nothing and knew nothing. One of the members of the firm, Donald Durant, was a member of the board of directors of the Kreuger enterprises. He had never attended a directors' meeting, and it is certain that he would have been no wiser had he done so.

During the last weeks of October, *Time* Magazine, young and not yet omniscient, also featured Kreuger on its cover – 'a great admirer of Cecil Rhodes'. Then a week later, as though to emphasize its faith in the New Era, it went on to Samuel Insull. (A fortnight after that, its youthful illusions shattered, the weekly news magazine gave the place of historic honour to Warden Lawes of Sing Sing.) In these same Indian summer days, *The Wall Street Journal* took notice of the official announcement that Andrew Mellon would remain in the cabinet at least until 1933 (there had been rumours that he might resign) and observed: 'Optimism again prevails ... the announcement ... did more to restore confidence than anything else.' In Germany Charles E. Mitchell announced that the 'industrial condition of the United States is absolutely sound', that too much attention was being paid to brokers' loans, and that 'nothing can arrest the upward movement'. On 15 October, as he sailed for home, he enlarged on the point: 'The markets generally are now in a healthy condition ... values have a sound basis in the general prosperity of our country.' That same evening Professor Irving Fisher made his historic announcement about the permanently high plateau and added, 'I expect to see the stock market a good deal higher than it is today within a few months.' Indeed, the only disturbing thing, in these October days, was the fairly steady downward drift in the market.

3

On Saturday, 19 October, Washington dispatches reported that Secretary of Commerce Lamont was having trouble finding the $100,000 in public funds that would be required to pay the upkeep of the yacht *Corsair* which J. P. Morgan had just given the government. (Morgan's deprivation was not extreme: a new $3,000,000 *Corsair* was being readied at Bath, Maine.) There were other and more compelling indications of an unaccustomed stringency. The papers told of a very weak market the day before – there were heavy declines on late trading, and the *Times* industrial average had dropped about 7 points. Steel had lost 7 points; General Electric, Westinghouse, and Montgomery Ward all lost 6. Meanwhile, that day's market was behaving very badly. In the second heaviest Saturday's trading in history, 3,488,100 shares were changing hands. At the close, the *Times* industrials were down 12 points. The blue chips were seriously off, and speculative favourites had gone into a nosedive. J. I. Case, for example, had fallen a full 40 points.

On Sunday the market was front-page news – the *Times* headline read, 'Stocks driven down as wave of selling engulfs the market', and the financial editor next day reported for perhaps the tenth time that the end had come. (He had learned, however, to hedge. 'For the time at any rate,' he said, 'Wall Street seemed to see the reality of things.') No immediate explanation of the break was forthcoming. The Federal Reserve had long been quiet. Babson had said nothing new. Hatry and the Massachusetts Department of Public Utilities were from a week to a month in the past. They became explanations only later.

The papers that Sunday carried three comments which were to become familiar in the days that followed. After Saturday's trading, it was noted, quite a few margin calls went out. This meant that the value of stock which the recipients held on margin had declined to the point where it was no longer sufficient collateral for the loan that had paid for it. The speculator was being asked for more cash.

The other two observations were more reassuring. The papers agreed, and this was also the informed view on Wall Street, that the worst was over. And it was predicted that on the following day the market would begin to receive organized support. Weakness, should it appear, would be tolerated no longer.

Never was there a phrase with more magic than 'organized support'. Almost immediately it was on every tongue and in every news story about the market. Organized support meant that powerful people would organize to keep prices of stocks at a reasonable level. Opinions differed as to who would organize this support. Some had in mind the big operators like Cutten, Durant, and Raskob. They, of all people, couldn't afford a collapse. Some thought of the bankers – Charles Mitchell had acted once before, and certainly if things got bad he would act again. Some had in mind the investment trusts. They held huge portfolios of common stocks, and obviously they could not afford to have them become cheap. Also, they had cash. So if stocks did become cheap the investment trusts would be in the market picking up bargains. This would mean that the bargains wouldn't last. With so many people wanting to avoid a further fall, a further fall would clearly be avoided.

In the ensuing weeks the Sabbath pause had a marked tendency to breed uneasiness and doubts and pessimism and a decision to get out on Monday. This, it seems certain, was what happened on Sunday, 20 October.

4

Monday, 21 October, was a very poor day. Sales totalled 6,091,870, the third greatest volume in history, and some tens of thousands who were watching the market throughout the country made a disturbing discovery. There was no way of telling what was happening. Previously on big days of the bull market the ticker had often fallen behind, and one didn't discover until well after the market closed how much richer he had become. But the experience with a falling market had been much more limited. Not since March had the ticker fallen seriously behind on declining values. Many now learned for the first time that they could be ruined, totally and forever, and not even know it. And if they were not ruined there was a strong tendency to imagine it. From the opening on the 21st the ticker lagged, and by noon it was an hour late. Not till an hour and forty minutes after the close of the market did it record the last transaction. Every ten minutes prices of selected bonds were printed on the bond ticker, but the wide divergence between these and the prices on the tape only added to the uneasiness – and to the growing conviction that it might be best to sell.

Things, though bad, were still not hopeless. Toward the end of Monday's trading the market rallied and final prices were above the lows for the day. The net losses were considerably less than on Saturday. Tuesday brought a somewhat shaky gain. As so often before, the market seemed to be showing its ability to come back. People got ready to record the experience as merely another setback of which there had been so many previously.

In doing so they were helped by the two men who now were recognized as Wall Street's official prophets. On Monday in New York, Professor Fisher said that the decline had represented only a 'shaking out of the lunatic fringe'. He went on to explain why he felt that the prices of stocks during the boom had not caught up with their real value and would go higher. Among other things, the market had not yet reflected the beneficent effects of prohibition which had made the American worker 'more productive and dependable'.

On Tuesday, Charles E. Mitchell dropped anchor in New York with the observation that 'the decline had gone too far'. (Time and sundry congressional and court proceedings were to show that Mr Mitchell had strong personal reasons for feeling that way.) He added that conditions were 'fundamentally sound', said again that too much attention had been paid to the large volume of brokers' loans, and concluded that the situation was one which would correct itself if left alone. However, another jarring suggestion came from Babson. He recommended selling stocks and buying gold.

By Wednesday, 23 October, the effect of this cheer was somehow dissipated. Instead of further gains there were heavy losses. The opening was quiet enough, but toward midmorning motor accessory stocks were sold heavily, and volume began to increase throughout the list. The last hour was quite phenomenal – 2,600,000 shares changed hands at rapidly declining prices. The *Times* industrial average for the day dropped from 415 to 384, giving up all of its gains since the end of the previous June. Tel and Tel lost 15 points; General Electric, 20; Westinghouse, 25; and J. I. Case, another 46. Again the ticker was far behind, and to add to the uncertainty an ice storm in the Middle West caused widespread disruption of communications. That afternoon and evening thousands of speculators decided to get out while – as they mistakenly supposed – the getting was good. Other thousands were told they had no choice but to get out unless they posted more collateral, for as the day's business came to an end an unprecedented volume of margin calls went out. Speaking in Washington, even Professor Fisher was fractionally less optimistic. He told a meeting of bankers that 'security values *in most instances* were not inflated'. However, he did not weaken on the unrealized efficiencies of prohibition.

The papers that night went to press with a souvenir of a fast departing era. Formidable advertisements announced subscription rights in a new offering of certificates in Aktiebolaget Kreuger and Toll at $23. There was also one bit of cheer. It was predicted that on the morrow the market would surely begin to receive 'organized support'.

## 5

Thursday, 24 October, is the first of the days which history – such as it is on the subject – identifies with the panic of 1929. Measured by disorder, fright, and confusion, it deserves to be so regarded. That day 12,894,650 shares changed hands, many of them at prices which shattered the dreams and the hopes of those who had owned them. Of all the mysteries of the Stock Exchange there is none so impenetrable as why there should be a buyer for everyone who seeks to sell. 24 October 1929, showed that what is mysterious is not inevitable. Often there were no buyers, and only after wide vertical declines could anyone be induced to bid.

The panic did not last all day. It was a phenomenon of the morning hours. The market opening itself was unspectacular, and for a while prices were firm. Volume, however, was very large, and soon prices began to sag. Once again the ticker dropped behind. Prices fell further and faster, and the ticker lagged more and more. By eleven o'clock the market had degenerated into a wild, mad scramble to sell. In the crowded boardrooms across the country the ticker told of a frightful collapse. But the selected quotations coming in over the bond ticker also showed that current values were far below the ancient history of the tape. The uncertainty led more and more people to try to sell. Others, no longer able to respond to margin calls, were sold out. By eleven-thirty the market had surrendered to blind, relentless fear. This, indeed, was panic.

Outside the Exchange in Broad Street a weird roar could be heard. A crowd gathered. Police Commissioner Grover Whalen became aware that something was happening and dispatched a special police detail to Wall Street to ensure the peace. More people came and waited, though apparently no one knew for what. A workman appeared atop one of the high buildings to accomplish some repairs, and the multitude assumed he was a would-be suicide and waited impatiently for him to jump. Crowds also formed around the branch offices of brokerage firms throughout the city and, indeed, throughout the country. Word of what was happening, or what was thought to be happening, was passed out by those who were within sight of the board or the Trans-Lux. An observer thought that people's expressions showed 'not so much suffering as a sort of horrified incredulity'.[1] Rumour after rumour swept Wall Street and those outlying wakes. Stocks were now selling for nothing. The Chicago and Buffalo Exchanges had closed. A suicide wave was in progress, and eleven well-known speculators had already killed themselves.

At twelve-thirty the officials of the New York Stock Exchange closed the visitors' gallery on the wild scenes below. One of the visitors who had just departed was showing his remarkable ability to be on hand with history. He was the former Chancellor of the Exchequer, Mr Winston Churchill. It was he who in 1925 returned Britain to the gold standard and the overvalued pound. Accordingly, he was responsible for the strain which sent Montagu Norman to plead in New York for easier money, which caused credit to be eased at the fatal time, which, in this academy view, in turn caused the boom. Now Churchill, it could be imagined, was viewing his awful handiwork.

There is no record of anyone's having reproached him. Economics was never his strong point, so (and wisely) it seems most unlikely that he reproached himself.

6

In New York at least the panic was over by noon. At noon the organized support appeared.

1. Edwin Lefèvre, 'The Little Fellow in Wall Street', *The Saturday Evening Post*, 4 January 1930.

At twelve o'clock reporters learned that a meeting was convening at 23 Wall Street at the offices of J. P. Morgan and Company. The word quickly passed as to who was there – Charles E. Mitchell, the Chairman of the Board of the National City Bank, Albert H. Wiggin, the Chairman of the Chase National Bank, William C. Potter, the President of the Guaranty Trust Company, Seward Prosser, the Chairman of the Bankers Trust Company, and the host, Thomas W. Lamont, the senior partner of Morgan's. According to legend, during the panic of 1907 the elder Morgan had brought to a halt the discussion of whether to save the tottering Trust Company of America by saying that the place to stop the panic was there. It was stopped. Now, twenty-two years later, that drama was being re-enacted. The elder Morgan was dead. His son was in Europe. But equally determined men were moving in. They were the nation's most powerful financiers. They had not yet been pilloried and maligned by New Dealers. The very news that they would act would release people from the fear to which they had surrendered.

It did. A decision was quickly reached to pool resources to support the market.[1] The meeting broke up, and Thomas Lamont met the reporters. His manner was described as serious, but his words were reassuring. In what Frederick Lewis Allen later called one of the most remarkable understatements of all time,[2] he told the newspapermen, 'There has been a little distress selling on the Stock Exchange.' He added that this was 'due to a technical condition of the market'

1. The amounts to be contributed or otherwise committed were never specified. Frederick Lewis Allen (*Only Yesterday*, pp. 329–30) says that each of the institutions, along with George F. Baker, Jr, of the First National, who later joined the pool, put up $40 million. This total – $240 million – seems much too large to be plausible. *The New York Times* subsequently suggested (9 March 1938) that the total was some $20 to $30 millions.

2. op. cit., p. 330.

rather than any fundamental cause, and told the newsmen that things were 'susceptible to betterment'. The bankers, he let it be known, had decided to better things.

Word had already reached the floor of the Exchange that the bankers were meeting, and the news ticker had spread the magic word afield. Prices firmed at once and started to rise. Then at one-thirty Richard Whitney appeared on the floor and went to the post where steel was traded. Whitney was perhaps the best-known figure on the floor. He was one of the group of men of good background and appropriate education who, in that time, were expected to manage the affairs of the Exchange. Currently he was vice-president of the Exchange, but in the absence of E. H. H. Simmons in Hawaii he was serving as acting president. What was much more important at the moment, he was known as floor trader for Morgan's and, indeed, his older brother was a Morgan partner.

As he made his way through the teeming crowd, Whitney appeared debonair and self-confident – some later described his manner as jaunty. (His own firm dealt largely in bonds, so it is improbable that he had been much involved in the turmoil of the morning.) At the Steel post he bid 205 for 10,000 shares. This was the price of the last sale, and the current bids were several points lower. In an operation that was totally devoid of normal commercial reticence, he got 200 shares and then left the rest of the order with the specialist. He continued on his way, placing similar orders for fifteen or twenty other stocks.

This was it. The bankers, obviously, had moved in. The effect was electric. Fear vanished and gave way to concern lest the new advance be missed. Prices boomed upward.

The bankers had, indeed, brought off a notable coup. Prices as they fell that morning kept crossing a large volume of stop-loss orders – orders calling for sales whenever a specified price was reached. Brokers had placed many of these orders for their own protection on the securities of customers who had not responded to calls for additional margin. Each of these stop-loss orders tripped more securities into the market and drove prices down further. Each spasm of liquidation thus ensured that another would follow. It was this literal chain reaction which the bankers checked, and they checked it decisively.

In the closing hour, selling orders continuing to come in from across the country turned the market soft once more. Still, in its own way, the recovery on Black Thursday was as remarkable as the selling that made it so black. The *Times* industrials were off only 12 points, or a little more than a third of the loss of the previous day. Steel, the stock that Whitney had singled out to start the recovery, had opened that morning at $205\frac{1}{2}$, a point or two above the previous close. At the lowest it was down to $193\frac{1}{2}$ for a 12-point loss.[1] Then it recovered to close at 206 for a surprising net gain of 2 points for this day. Montgomery Ward, which had opened at 83 and gone to 50, came back to 74. General Electric was at one point 32 points below its opening price and then came back 25 points. On the Curb, Goldman Sachs Trading Corporation opened at 81, dropped to 65, and then came back to 80. J. I. Case, maintaining a reputation for eccentric behaviour that had brought much risk capital into the threshing machine business, made a net gain of 7 points for the day. Many had good reason to be grateful to the financial leaders of Wall Street.

## 7

Not everyone could be grateful, to be sure. Across the country people were only dimly aware of the improvement. By early afternoon, when the market started up, the ticker was hours behind. Although the spot quotations on the bond ticker

1. Quotations have normally been rounded to the nearest whole number in this history. The steel quotation on this day seems to call for an exception.

showed the improvement, the ticker itself continued to grind out the most dismal of news. And the news on the ticker was what counted. To many, many watchers it meant that they had been sold out and that their dream – in fact, their brief reality – of opulence had gone glimmering, together with home, car, furs, jewellery, and reputation. That the market, after breaking them, had recovered was the most chilling of comfort.

It was eight and a half minutes past seven that night before the ticker finished recording the day's misfortunes. In the boardrooms speculators who had been sold out since morning sat silently watching the tape. The habit of months or years, however idle it had now become, could not be abandoned at once. Then, as the final trades were registered, sorrowfully or grimly, according to their nature, they made their way out into the gathering night.

In Wall Street itself lights blazed from every office as clerks struggled to come abreast of the day's business. Messengers and boardroom boys, caught up in the excitement and untroubled by losses, went skylarking through the streets until the police arrived to quell them. Representatives of thirty-five of the largest wire houses assembled at the offices of Hornblower and Weeks and told the press on departing that the market was 'fundamentally sound' and 'technically in better condition than it has been in months'. It was the unanimous view of those present that the worst had passed. The host firm dispatched a market letter which stated that 'commencing with today's trading the market should start laying the foundation for the constructive advance which we believe will characterize 1930'. Charles E. Mitchell announced that the trouble was 'purely technical' and that 'fundamentals remained unimpaired'. Senator Carter Glass said that trouble was due largely to Charles E. Mitchell. Senator Wilson of Indiana attributed the crash to Democratic resistance to a higher tariff.

8

On Friday and Saturday trading continued heavy – just under six million on Friday and over two million at the short session on Saturday. Prices, on the whole, were steady – the averages were a trifle up on Friday but slid off on Saturday. It was thought that the bankers were able to dispose of most of the securities they had acquired while shoring up the market on Thursday. Not only were things better, but everyone was clear as to who had made them so. The bankers had shown both their courage and their power, and the people applauded warmly and generously. The financial community, the *Times* said, now felt 'secure in the knowledge that the most powerful banks in the country stood ready to prevent a recurrence [of panic]'. As a result it had 'relaxed its anxiety'.

Perhaps never before or since have so many people taken the measure of economic prospects and found them so favourable as in the two days following the Thursday disaster. The optimism even included a note of self-congratulation. Colonel Ayres in Cleveland thought that no other country could have come through such a bad crash so well. Others pointed out that the prospects for business were good and that the stock market debacle would not make them any less favourable. No one knew, but it cannot be stressed too frequently, that for effective incantation knowledge is neither necessary nor assumed.

Eugene M. Stevens, the President of the Continental Illinois Bank, said, 'There is nothing in the business situation to justify any nervousness.' Walter Teagle said there had been no 'fundamental change' in the oil business to justify concern; Charles M. Schwab said that the steel business had been making 'fundamental progress' toward stability and added that this 'fundamentally sound condition' was responsible for the prosperity of the industry; Samuel Vauclain, Chairman of the

Baldwin Locomotive Works, declared that 'fundamentals are sound'; President Hoover said that 'the fundamental business of the country, that is production and distribution of commodities, is on a sound and prosperous basis'. President Hoover was asked to say something more specific about the market – for example, that stocks were now cheap – but he refused.[1]

Many others joined in. Howard C. Hopson, the head of Associated Gas and Electric, omitted the standard reference to fundamentals and thought it was 'undoubtedly beneficial to the business interests of the country to have the gambling type of speculator eliminated'. (Mr Hopson, himself a speculator, although more of the sure-thing type, was also eliminated in due course.) A Boston investment trust took space in *The Wall Street Journal* to say, 'S-T-E-A-D-Y Everybody! Calm thinking is in order. Heed the words of America's greatest bankers.' A single dissonant note, though great in portent, went unnoticed. Speaking in Poughkeepsie, Governor Franklin D. Roosevelt criticized the 'fever of speculation'.

On Sunday there were sermons suggesting that a certain measure of divine retribution had been visited on the Republic and that it had not been entirely unmerited. People had lost sight of spiritual values in their single-minded pursuit of riches. Now they had had their lesson.

Almost everyone believed that the heavenly knuckle-rapping was over and that speculation could be now resumed in earnest. The papers were full of the prospects for next week's market.

Stocks, it was agreed, were again cheap and accordingly there would be a heavy rush to buy. Numerous stories from the

1. This was stated by Garet Garrett in *The Saturday Evening Post* (28 December 1929) and it is generally confirmed by Mr Hoover in his memoirs. According to Mr Garrett the bankers' consortium asked the President for the statement, which suggests that the reassurance, like the support, was tolerably well organized.

brokerage houses, some of them possibly inspired, told of a fabulous volume of buying orders which was piling up in anticipation of the opening of the market. In a concerted advertising campaign in Monday's papers, stock market firms urged the wisdom of picking up these bargains promptly. 'We believe', said one house, 'that the investor who purchases securities at this time with the discrimination that is always a condition of prudent investing, may do so with utmost confidence.' On Monday the real disaster began.

# CHAPTER VII

# THINGS BECOME MORE SERIOUS

## I

IN the autumn of 1929 the New York Stock Exchange, under roughly its present constitution, was 112 years old. During this lifetime it had seen some difficult days. On 18 September 1873, the firm of Jay Cooke and Company failed, and, as a more or less direct result, so did fifty-seven other Stock Exchange firms in the next few weeks. On 23 October 1907, call money rates reached one hundred and twenty-five per cent in the panic of that year. On 16 September 1920 – the autumn months are the off-season in Wall Street – a bomb exploded in front of Morgan's next door, killing thirty people and injuring a hundred more.

A common feature of all these earlier troubles was that, having happened, they were over. The worst was reasonably recognizable as such. The singular feature of the great crash of 1929 was that the worst continued to worsen. What looked one day like the end proved on the next day to have been only the beginning. Nothing could have been more ingeniously designed to maximize the suffering, and also to ensure that as few as possible escaped the common misfortune. The fortunate speculator who had funds to answer the first margin call presently got another and equally urgent one, and if he met that there would still be another. In the end all the money he had was extracted from him and lost. The man with the smart money, who was safely out of the market when the first crash came, naturally went back in to pick up bargains. (Not only were a recorded 12,894,650 shares sold on 24 October; precisely the same number were bought.) The bargains then suffered a ruinous fall. Even the man who waited out all of October and all of November, who saw the volume of trading return to normal and saw Wall Street become as placid as a produce market, and who then bought common stocks would see their value drop to a third or a fourth of the purchase price in the next twenty-four months. The Coolidge bull market was a remarkable phenomenon. The ruthlessness of its liquidation was, in its own way, equally remarkable.

2

Monday, 28 October, was the first day on which this process of climax and anticlimax *ad infinitum* began to reveal itself. It was another terrible day. Volume was huge, although below the previous Thursday – nine and a quarter million shares as compared with nearly thirteen. But the losses were far more severe. The *Times* industrials were down 49 points for the day. General Electric was off 48; Westinghouse, 34; Tel and Tel, 34. Steel went down 18 points. Indeed, the decline on this one day was greater than that of all the preceding week of panic. Once again a late ticker left everyone in ignorance of what was happening, save that it was bad.

On this day there was no recovery. At one-ten Charles E. Mitchell was observed going into Morgan's, and the news ticker carried the magic word. Steel rallied and went from 194 to 198. But Richard Whitney did not materialize. It seems probable in light of later knowledge that Mitchell was on the way to float a personal loan. The market weakened again, and in the last hour a phenomenal three million shares – a big day's business before and ever since – changed hands at rapidly falling prices.

At four-thirty in the afternoon the bankers assembled once more at Morgan's, and they remained in session until six-thirty. They were described as taking a philosophical attitude, and they told the press that the situation 'retained hopeful features', although these were not specified. But the statement they released after the meeting made clear what had been discussed for the two hours. It was no part of the bankers' purpose, the statement said, to maintain any particular level of prices or to protect anyone's profit. Rather the aim was to have an orderly market, one in which offers would be met by bids at some price. The bankers were only concerned that 'air holes', as Mr Lamont dubbed them, did not appear.

Like many lesser men, Mr Lamont and his colleagues had suddenly found themselves overcommitted on a falling market. The time had come to go short on promises. Support, organized or otherwise, could not contest with the overwhelming, pathological desire to sell. The meeting had considered how to liquidate the commitment to support the market without adding to the public perturbation.

The formula that was found was a chilling one. On Thursday, Whitney had supported prices and protected profits – or stopped losses. This was what people wanted. To the man who held stock on margin, disaster had only one face and that was falling prices. But now prices were to be allowed to fall. The speculator's only comfort, henceforth, was that his ruin would be accomplished in an orderly and becoming manner.

There were no recriminations at the time. Our political life favours the extremes of speech; the man who is gifted in the arts of abuse is bound to be a notable, if not always a great figure. In business, things are different. Here we are surprisingly gentle and forbearing. Even preposterous claims or excuses are normally taken, at least for all public purposes, at the face value. On the evening of the 28th no one any longer could feel 'secure in the knowledge that the most powerful banks stood ready to prevent a recurrence' of panic. The market had reasserted itself as an impersonal force beyond the power of any person to control, and, while this is the way markets are supposed to be, it was horrible. But no one assailed the bankers for letting the people down. There was even some talk that on the next day the market might receive organized support.

## 8

Tuesday, 29 October, was the most devastating day in the history of the New York stock market, and it may have been the most devastating day in the history of markets. It combined all of the bad features of all of the bad days before. Volume was immensely greater than on Black Thursday; the drop in prices was almost as great as on Monday. Uncertainty and alarm were as great as on either.

Selling began as soon as the market opened and in huge volume. Great blocks of stock were offered for what they would bring; in the first half-hour sales were at a 33,000,000-a-day rate. The air holes, which the bankers were to close, opened wide. Repeatedly and in many issues there was a plethora of selling orders and no buyers at all. The stock of White Sewing Machine Company, which had reached a high of 48 in the months preceding, had closed at 11 the night before. During the day someone – according to Frederick Lewis Allen it was thought to have been a bright messenger boy for the Exchange – had the happy idea of entering a bid for a block of stock at a dollar a share. In the absence of any other bid he got it.[1] Once again, of course, the ticker lagged – at the close it was two and a half hours behind. By then, 16,410,030 sales had been recorded on the New York Stock Exchange – some certainly went unrecorded – or more than three times the number that was once considered a fabulously big day. The *Times* industrial averages were down 43 points, cancelling all of the gains of the twelve wonderful months preceding.

1. *Only Yesterday*, p. 333.

The losses would have been worse had there not been a closing rally. Thus Steel, for which Whitney had bid 205 on Thursday, reached 167 during the course of the day, although it rallied to 174 at the close. American Can opened at 130, dropped to 110, and rose to 120. Westinghouse opened at 131 – on 3 September it had closed at 286 – and dropped to 100. Then it rallied to 126. But the worst thing that happened on this terrible day was to the investment trusts. Not only did they go down, but it became apparent that they could go practically to nothing. Goldman Sachs Trading Corporation had closed at 60 the night before. During the day it dropped to 35 and closed at that level, off by not far short of half. Blue Ridge, its offspring once removed, on which the magic of leverage was now working in reverse, did much worse. Early in September it had sold at 24. By 24 October it was down to 12, but it resisted rather well the misfortunes of that day and the day following. On the morning of 29 October it opened at 10 and promptly slipped to 3, giving up more than two-thirds of its value. It recovered later but other investment trusts did less well; their stock couldn't be sold at all.

The worst day on Wall Street came eventually to an end. Once again the lights blazed all night. Members of the Exchange, their employees, and the employees of the Stock Exchange by now were reaching the breaking point from strain and fatigue. In this condition they faced the task of recording and handling the greatest volume of transactions ever. All of this was without the previous certainty that things might get better. They might go on getting worse. In one house an employee fainted from exhaustion, was revived, and put back to work again.

## 4

In the first week the slaughter had been of the innocents. During this second week there is some evidence that it was the well-to-do and the wealthy who were being subjected to a levelling process comparable in magnitude and suddenness to that presided over a decade before by Lenin. The size of the blocks of stock which were offered suggested that big speculators were selling or being sold. Another indication came from the boardrooms. A week before they were crowded, now they were nearly empty. Those now in trouble had facilities for suffering in private.

The bankers met twice on the 29th – at noon and again in the evening. There was no suggestion that they were philosophical. This was hardly remarkable because, during the day, an appalling rumour had swept the Exchange. It was that the bankers' pool, so far from stabilizing the market, was actually selling stocks! The prestige of the bankers had in truth been falling even more rapidly than the market. After the evening session, Mr Lamont met the press with the disenchanting task of denying that they had been liquidating securities – or participating in a bear raid. After explaining again, somewhat redundantly in view of the day's events, that it was not the purpose of the bankers to maintain a particular level of prices, he concluded: 'The group has continued and will continue in a cooperative way to support the market and has not been a seller of stocks.' In fact, as later intelligence revealed, Albert H. Wiggin of the Chase was personally short at the time to the tune of some millions. His cooperative support, which if successful would have cost him heavily, must have had an interesting element of ambivalence.

So ended the organized support. The phrase recurred during the next few days, but no one again saw in it any ground for hope. Few men ever lost position so rapidly as did the New York bankers in the five days from 24 October to 29 October. The crash on 24 October was the signal for corporations and out-of-town banks, which had been luxuriating in the ten per cent and more rate of interest, to recall their money from Wall

Street. Between 23 October and 30 October, as values fell and margin accounts were liquidated, the volume of brokers' loans fell by over a billion. But the corporations and the out-of-town banks responded to the horrifying news from New York – although, in fact, their funds were never seriously endangered – by calling home over two billions. The New York banks stepped into the gaping hole that was left by these summer financiers, and during that first week of crisis they increased their loans by about a billion. This was a bold step. Had the New York banks succumbed to the general fright, a money panic would have been added to the other woes. Stocks would have been dumped because their owners could not have borrowed money at any price to carry them. To prevent this was a considerable achievement for which all who owned stocks should have been thankful. But the banks received no credit. People remembered only that they had bravely undertaken to stem the price collapse and had failed.

Despite a flattering supposition to the contrary, people come readily to terms with power. There is little reason to think that the power of the great bankers, while they were assumed to have it, was much resented. But as the ghosts of numerous tyrants, from Julius Caesar to Benito Mussolini, will testify, people are very hard on those who, having had power, lose it or are destroyed. Then anger at past arrogance is joined with contempt for present weakness. The victim or his corpse is made to suffer all available indignities.

Such was the fate of the bankers. For the next decade they were fair game for congressional committees, courts, the press, and the comedians. The great pretensions and the great failures of these days were a cause. A banker need not be popular; indeed, a good banker in a healthy capitalist society should probably be much disliked. People do not wish to trust their money to a hail-fellow-well-met but to a misanthrope who can say no. However, a banker must not seem futile, ineffective, or vaguely foolish. In contrast with the stern power of Morgan in 1907, that was precisely how his successors seemed, or were made to seem, in 1929.

The failure of the bankers did not leave the community entirely without constructive leadership. There was Mayor James J. Walker. Appearing before a meeting of motion picture exhibitors on that Tuesday, he appealed to them to 'show pictures which will reinstate courage and hope in the hearts of the people'.

## 5

On the Exchange itself, there was a strong feeling that courage and hope might best be restored by just closing up for a while. This feeling had, in fact, been gaining force for several days. Now it derived support from the simple circumstance that everyone was badly in need of sleep. Employees of some Stock Exchange firms had not been home for days. Hotel rooms in downtown New York were at a premium, and restaurants in the financial area had gone on to a fifteen- and twenty-hour day. Nerves were bad, and mistakes were becoming increasingly common. After the close of trading on Tuesday, a broker found a large waste basket of unexecuted orders which he had set aside for early attention and had totally forgotten.[1] One customer, whose margin account was impaired, was sold out twice. A number of firms needed some time to see if they were still solvent. There were, in fact, no important failures by Stock Exchange firms during these days, although one firm had reported itself bankrupt as the result of a clerical error by an employee who was in the last stages of fatigue.[2]

1. Allen, op. cit., p. 334.
2. *The Work of the Stock Exchange in the Panic of 1929*, an address by Richard Whitney before the Boston Association of Stock Exchange Firms. Boston, 10 June 1930, pp. 16, 17. Whitney's account, below, of the events of 29 October and thereafter is from the same source.

Yet to close the Exchange was a serious matter. It might somehow signify that stocks had lost all their value, with consequences no one could foresee. In any case, securities would immediately become a badly frozen asset. This would be hard on wholly solvent investors who might need to realize on them or use them as collateral. And sooner or later a new 'gutter' market would develop in which individuals would informally dispose of stocks to those increasingly exceptional individuals who still wanted to buy them.

In 1929 the New York Stock Exchange was in principle a sovereignty of its members. Apart from the general statutes relating to the conduct of business and the prevention of fraud, it was subject to no important state or federal regulation. This meant a considerable exercise of self-government. Legislation governing the conduct of trading had to be kept under review and enforced. Stocks had to be approved for listing. The building and other facilities of the Exchange had to be managed. As with the United States Congress, most of this work was done in committees. (These, in turn, were dominated by a somewhat smaller group of members who were expected and accustomed to run things.) A decision to close the Exchange had to be taken by the Governing Committee, a body of about forty members. The mere knowledge that this body was meeting would almost certainly have an unfavourable effect on the market.

Nonetheless, at noon on Tuesday, the 29th, a meeting was held. The members of the committee left the floor in twos and threes and went, not to the regular meeting room, but to the office of the President of the Stock Clearing Corporation directly below the trading floor. Some months later, Acting President Whitney described the session with considerable graphic talent. 'The office they met in was never designed for large meetings of this sort, with the result that most of the Governors were compelled to stand, or to sit on tables. As the meeting proceeded, panic was raging overhead on the floor. Every few minutes the latest prices were announced, with quotations moving swiftly and irresistibly downwards. The feeling of those present was revealed by their habit of continually lighting cigarettes, taking a puff or two, putting them out and lighting new ones – a practice which soon made the narrow room blue with smoke and extremely stuffy.'

The result of these nervous deliberations was a decision to meet again in the evening. By evening the late rally had occurred, and it was decided to stay open for another day. The next day a further formula was hit upon. The Exchange would stay open. But it would have some special holidays and then go on short hours, and this would be announced just as soon as the market seemed strong enough to stand it.

Many still wanted to close. Whitney said later, although no doubt with some exaggeration, that in the days to come 'the authorities of the Exchange led the life of hunted things, until [eventually] the desirability of holding the market open became apparent to all!'.

## 6

The next day those forces were at work which on occasion bring salvation precisely when salvation seems impossible. Stocks rose wonderfully, miraculously, though still on enormous volume. The *Times* industrials were up 31 points for the day, thus recouping a large part of the terrible losses of the day before. Why this recovery occurred no one will ever know. Organized support can have no credit. Organized reassurance has a somewhat better claim. On the evening of the 29th, Dr Julius Klein, Assistant Secretary of Commerce, friend of President Hoover, and the senior apostle of the official economic view, took to the radio to remind the country that President Hoover had said that the 'fundamental business of the country' was sound. He added firmly, 'The main point which I want to emphasize is the fundamental soundness of [the] great mass of economic activities.' On Wednesday, Waddill Catchings, of Goldman, Sachs, announced on return from a western trip that general business conditions were 'unquestionably fundamentally sound'. (The same, by then, could not unquestionably be said of all Goldman, Sachs.) Arthur Brisbane told Hearst readers: 'To comfort yourself, if you lost, think of the people living near Mount Pelee, ordered to abandon their homes.'

Most important, perhaps, from Pocantico Hills came the first public statement by John D. Rockefeller in several decades. So far as the record shows, it was spontaneous. However, someone in Wall Street – perhaps someone who knew that another appeal to President Hoover to say something specifically encouraging about stocks would be useless – may have realized that a statement from Rockefeller would, if anything, be better. The statement ran: 'Believing that fundamental conditions of the country are sound . . . my son and I have for some days been purchasing sound common stocks.' The statement was widely applauded, although Eddie Cantor, describing himself as Comedian, Author, Statistician, and Victim, said later, 'Sure, who else had any money left?'[1]

The accepted Wall Street explanation of Wednesday's miracle was not the reassurance but the dividend news of the day before. This also, without much question, was somewhat organized. U.S. Steel had declared an extra dividend; American Can had not only declared an extra but had increased its regular dividend. These errant sunbeams were deeply welcome in the dark canyons of lower Manhattan.

Just before the Rockefeller statement arrived, things looked good enough on the Exchange so that Richard Whitney felt safe in announcing that the market would not open until noon the

1. *Caught Short! A Saga of Wailing Wall Street*, New York (Simon and Schuster), 1929 A.C. (After Crash), p. 31.

following day (Thursday) and that on Friday and Saturday it would stay shut. The announcement was greeted by cheers. Nerves were clearly past the breaking point. On La Salle Street in Chicago a boy exploded a firecracker. Like wildfire the rumour spread that gangsters whose margin accounts had been closed out were shooting up the street. Several squads of police arrived to make them take their losses like honest men. In New York the body of a commission merchant was fished out of the Hudson. The pockets contained $9.40 in change and some margin calls.

## 7

At the short session of three hours on Thursday, 31 October, well over seven million shares were traded, and the market made another good gain. The *Times* industrials were up 21 points. The weekly return of the Federal Reserve Bank showed a drop in brokers' loans by more than a billion, the largest weekly drop on record. Margin requirements had already been cut to twenty-five per cent; now the Federal Reserve Banks lowered the rediscount rate from six to five per cent. The Reserve Banks also launched vigorous open-market purchases of bonds to ease money rates and liberalize the supply of credit. The boom had collapsed; the restraint that had previously been contemplated could now give way to a policy of active encouragement to the market. On all these happy portents the market closed down for Friday, Saturday, and Sunday. They were not days of rest. Brokerage offices were fully staffed, and the Exchange floor was open for completion of trades and also for straightening out innumerable misunderstandings and mistakes. It was noted that on Friday a visitor to the galleries could not have told the market was suspended.

The weekend brought one piece of bad news. That was the announcement on Saturday of the failure of the $20,000,000 Foshay enterprises of Minneapolis. Foshay owned utilities in some twelve states, Canada, Mexico, and Central America, and an assortment of hotels, flour mills, banks, manufacturing and retail establishments wherever he had happened to buy them. The 32-storey obelisk, commemorating the enterprise, which still dominates the Minneapolis skyline, had been opened with fitting ceremony by Secretary of War James W. Good, only in August. (Secretary Good had referred to it as the 'Washington Monument of the North-west.'[1]) By all but the most technical of considerations, Foshay was bankrupt at that festive time. His survival depended on his ability to continue merchandising stock to the public. The market crash eliminated this source of revenue and made him dependent on the wholly inadequate earnings of his enterprises.

On all other fronts the news was all good. Alfred P. Sloan, Jr, President of the General Motors Corporation, said: 'Business is sound.' The Ford Motor Company emphasized a similar conviction by announcing a general reduction in its prices: '... we feel that such a step is the best contribution that could be made to assure a continuation of good business'. The Roadster was cut from $450 to $435; the Phaeton from $460 to $440; the Tudor Sedan from $525 to $500. For the three days that the market was closed the papers carried stories of the accumulation of buying orders and, in some indefinable way, the stories had a greater ring of conviction than the week before. The market, after all, had closed after an excellent two-day rally. As *Barron's* pointed out, it could now be believed that stocks were selling 'ex-hopes and romance'. On Monday, the Commercial National Bank and Trust Company took five columns in the *Times* to advertise '... our belief and conviction that the general industrial and business condition of the country is fundamentally sound and is essentially unimpaired'.

That day the market started on another ghastly slump.

1. *Investment News*, 16 October 1929, p. 538.

## 8

Over the weekend the financial community had almost certainly been persuaded by its own organized and spontaneous efforts at cheer. The paper described the reaction of professional Wall Street to Monday's market as one of stunned surprise, disbelief, and shock. Volume was smaller than the week before, but still well above six million. The whole list was weak; individual issues made big losses; the *Times* industrials were down 22 points for the day. Compared with anything but the week before, this was very bad. When measured against the bright hopes for that day, it was most distressing.

Explanations varied. The rumour recurred that the 'organized support' was selling stocks, and Mr Lamont, on meeting the press, added a minor footnote to this now completed story. He said he didn't know – the organized support was really not that well organized. The most plausible explanation is that everyone was feeling cheerful but the public. As before and later, the weekend had been a time of thought, and out of thought had come pessimism and a decision to sell. So, as on other Mondays, no matter how cheerful the superficial portents, the selling orders poured in in volume.

By now it was also evident that the investment trusts, once considered a buttress of the high plateau and a built-in defence against collapse, were really a profound source of weakness. The leverage, of which people only a fortnight before had spoken so knowledgeably and even affectionately, was now fully in reverse. With remarkable celerity it removed all of the value from the common stock of a trust. As before, the case of a typical trust, a small one, is worth contemplating. Let it be supposed that it had securities in the hands of the public which had a market value of $10,000,000 in early October. Of this, half was in common stock, half in bonds and preferred stock. These securities were fully covered by the current market value of the securities owned. In other words, the trust's portfolio contained securities with a market value also of $10,000,000.

A representative portfolio of securities owned by such a trust would, in the early days of November, have declined in value by perhaps half. (Values of many of these securities by later standards would still be handsome; on 4 November, the low for Tel and Tel was still 233, for General Electric it was 234, and for Steel 183.) The new portfolio value, $5,000,000, would be only enough to cover the prior claim on assets of the bonds and preferred stock. The common stock would have nothing behind it. Apart from expectations, which were by no means bright, it was now worthless.

This geometrical ruthlessness was not exceptional. On the contrary, it was everywhere at work on the stock of the leverage trusts. By early November, the stock of most of them had become virtually unsaleable. To make matters worse, many of them were traded on the Curb or the out-of-town exchanges where buyers were few and the markets thin.

Never was there a time when more people wanted more money more urgently than in those days. The word that a man had 'got caught' by the markets was the signal for his creditors to descend on him like locusts. Many who were having trouble meeting their margin calls wanted to sell some stocks so they could hold the rest and thus salvage something from their misfortunes. But such people now found that their investment trust securities could not be sold for any appreciable sum and perhaps not at all. They were forced, as a result, to realize on their good securities. Standard stocks like Steel, General Motors, Tel and Tel were thus dumped on the market in abnormal volume, with the effect on prices that had already been fully revealed. The great investment trust boom had ended in a unique manifestation of Gresham's Law in which the bad stocks were driving out the good.

The stabilizing effects of the huge cash resources of the

investment trusts had also proved a mirage. In the early autumn the cash and liquid resources of the investment trusts were large. Many trusts had been attracted by the handsome returns in the call market. (The speculative circle had been closed. People who speculated in the stock of investment trusts were in effect investing in companies which provided the funds to finance their own speculation.) But now, as reverse leverage did its work, investment trust managements were much more concerned over the collapse in the value of their own stock than over the adverse movements in the stock list as a whole. The investment trusts had invested heavily in each other. As a result the fall in Blue Ridge hit Shenandoah, and the resulting collapse in Shenandoah was even more horrible for the Goldman Sachs Trading Corporation.

Under these circumstances, many of the trusts used their available cash in a desperate effort to support their own stock. However, there was a vast difference between buying one's stock now when the public wanted to sell and buying during the previous spring – as Goldman Sachs Trading Corporation had done – when the public wanted to buy and the resulting competition had sent prices higher and higher. Now the cash went out and the stock came in, and prices were either not perceptibly affected or not for long. What six months before had been a brilliant financial manoeuvre was now a form of fiscal self-immolation. In the last analysis, the purchase by a firm of its own stock is the exact opposite of the sale of stocks. It is by the sale of stock that firms ordinarily grow.

However, none of this was immediately apparent. If one has been a financial genius, faith in one's genius does not dissolve at once. To the battered but unbowed genius, support of the stock of one's own company still seemed a bold, imaginative, and effective course. Indeed, it seemed the only alternative to slow but certain death. So to the extent that their cash resources allowed, the managements of the trusts chose faster, though equally certain death. They bought their own worthless stock. Men have been swindled by other men on many occasions. The autumn of 1929 was, perhaps, the first occasion when men succeeded on a large scale in swindling themselves.

The time has now come to complete the chronicle of the last days of the crisis.

## 9

Tuesday, 5 November, was election day, and the market was closed all day. In the New York mayoralty race, the Democratic incumbent, James J. Walker, scored a landslide victory over his Republican opponent, F. H. La Guardia, who had been soundly denounced by the Democrats as a socialist. Babson, in a statement, called for poise, discernment, judicious courage, and old-fashioned common sense. On Wednesday the market reopened for the first of a new series of short sessions of three hours. These were the compromise on the question of closing which had been reached the previous week. Nearly six million shares were traded in this session or the equivalent of ten million shares on a full day. There was another sickening slide. U.S. Steel opened at 181, and, by what one paper called a succession of 'feverish dips', went to 165. Auburn Automobile lost 66 points; Otis Elevator lost 45. The *Times* industrials were off 37 points for the day, or only 6 points less than on the terrible Tuesday eight days earlier. Where would it all end?

There was also disturbing news from beyond the market. Fundamentals seemed to be turning sour. The week's figures on carloadings showed a heavy drop as compared with the year before. The steel rate was significantly down from the preceding week. More serious, the slump had extended to the commodity markets. On previous days these had reacted sympathetically with the stock market. On this Wednesday they had troubles of their own. Cotton was sharply off in the heaviest trading in weeks. References were made to 'panic' in the wheat market when the price dropped vertically at noon.

On Thursday the stock market was steady to higher, but on Friday it took a small drop. People had another weekend of contemplation. This time there was no talk of an accumulation of buying orders; indeed, there was little good news of any kind. On Monday, 11 November, came another drastic slump. For the next two days trading was heavy – the Exchange was still on short hours – and prices went down still more. In these three days, 11, 12, and 13 November, the *Times* industrials lost another 50 points.

Of all the days of the crash, these without doubt were the dreariest. Organized support had failed. For the moment even organized reassurance had been abandoned. All that could be managed was some sardonic humour. It was noted that the margin calls going out by Western Union that week carried a small sticker: 'Remember them at home with a cheery Thanksgiving telegram, the American way for this American day.' Clerks in downtown hotels were said to be asking guests whether they wished the room for sleeping or jumping. Two men jumped hand-in-hand from a high window in the Ritz. They had a joint account. *The Wall Street Journal*, becoming biblical, told its readers: 'Verily, I say, let the fear of the market be the law of thy life, and abide by the words of the bond salesman.' The financial editor of the *Times*, who by this time showed signs of being satisfied with the crash and perhaps even of feeling that it had gone too far, said: 'Probably none of the present generation will be able to speak again . . . of a "healthy reaction". There are many signs that the phrase is entirely out of date.'

# CHAPTER VIII

# AFTERMATH I

I

IN the week or so following Black Thursday, the London penny press told delightedly of the scenes in downtown New York. Speculators were hurling themselves from windows; pedestrians picked their way delicately between the bodies of fallen financiers. The American correspondent for the *Economist* wrote an indignant column for his paper protesting against this picture of imaginary carnage.

In the United States the suicide wave that followed the stock market crash is also part of the legend of 1929. In fact, there was none. For several years before 1929, the suicide rate had been gradually rising. It continued to increase in that year, with a further and much sharper increase in 1930, 1931, and 1932 – years when there were many things besides the stock market to cause people to conclude that life was no longer worth living. The statistics for New Yorkers, who might be assumed to have had a special propensity for self-destruction, derived from their propinquity to the market, show only a slight deviation from those for the country as a whole. Since the suicide myth is so well established, it may be useful to give the detailed figures, which are shown on the following page.

Since the market crash took place late in the year, there could have been a substantial increase in suicides in late October and thereafter which still would not be great enough to affect the figures for the year as a whole. However, figures on the causes of death by months are also available for 1929.[1]

1. I am grateful to the custodians of vital statistics in the Department of Health, Education and Welfare for tracking down these figures for me. They are from *Mortality Statistics, 1929* (Washington: Department of Commerce, Bureau of the Census).

These show that the number of suicides in October and November was comparatively low – in October, 1,331 suicides in all the United States, and in November, 1,344. In only three other months – January, February, and September – did fewer people destroy themselves. During the summer months, when the market was doing beautifully, the number of suicides was substantially higher.

NUMBER OF SUICIDES PER 100,000 OF POPULATION
1925–34

| Year | For Registration Area* | For New York City |
|------|------------------------|-------------------|
| 1925 | 12·1 | 14·4 |
| 1926 | 12·8 | 13·7 |
| 1927 | 13·3 | 15·7 |
| 1928 | 13·6 | 15·7 |
| 1929 | 14·0 | 17·0 |
| 1930 | 15·7 | 18·7 |
| 1931 | 16·8 | 19·7 |
| 1932 | 17·4 | 21·3 |
| 1933 | 15·9 | 18·5 |
| 1934 | 14·9 | 17·0 |

* The Registration Area is the part of the country – most of it – wherein causes of death are duly reported. Data are from *Vital Statistics: Special Reports, 1–45, 1935.* Washington (Department of Commerce, Bureau of the Census), 1937.

One can only guess how the suicide myth became established. Like alcoholics and gamblers, broken speculators are supposed to have a propensity for self-destruction. At a time when broken speculators were plentiful, the newspapers and the public may have simply supplied the corollary. Alternatively, suicides that in other times would have evoked the question, 'Why do you suppose he did it?' now had the motive assigned automatically: 'The poor fellow was caught in the crash.' Finally, it must be noted that, although suicides did not increase sharply either in the months of the crash or in 1929 as a whole, the rate did rise in the later depression years. In memory some of these tragedies may have been moved back a year or two to the time of the stock market crash.

The weight of the evidence suggests that the newspapers and the public merely seized on such suicides as occurred to show that people were reacting appropriately to their misfortune. Enough deaths could be related in one way or another to the market to serve. Beginning soon after Black Thursday, stories of violent self-destruction began to appear in the papers with some regularity. Curiously, though another myth runs strongly to the contrary, few people in these days followed the classic method of jumping from a high window. One would-be suicide jumped into the Schuylkill River, although he changed his mind when he hit the water and was fished out. The head of the Rochester Gas and Electric Company took gas. Another martyr dipped himself in gasoline and touched himself off. He not only made good his escape from his margin calls, but took his wife with him. There was also the suicide of J. J. Riordan.

Riordan's death made large headlines in the newspapers on Sunday, 10 November. The papers obviously had sensed a story not only in his death itself, but also in the manner of its announcement. Riordan was a widely-known and popular figure among New York Democrats. He had been treasurer of one of Mayor Walker's campaigns and also of one of Al Smith's. He and Smith were close friends and business associates. Al Smith was a member of the board of directors of the recently-organized County Trust Company, of which Riordan was the president.

On Friday, 8 November, Riordan went to his bank, took a pistol from a teller's cage, went home, and shot himself. Al Smith was notified, and his sorrow over the death of his friend was not diminished by the knowledge that the news might start a serious run on their bank. A medical examiner was called but further notification was withheld until the following day (Saturday) at noon, when the bank had closed for the weekend. There had been a long wake through which the distinguished mourners had kept one eye on the corpse and the other on the clock.

The medical examiner first implied that he had postponed notification out of a feeling of deep responsibility for depositors of the Country Trust. This was a formidable exercise of discretion; carried to its logical conclusion, it meant that all deaths would have to be weighed by the attending doctor for their financial consequences. Later it was tacitly conceded that the decision was Al Smith's. So great was Smith's prestige – and also the general nervousness – that the action was not questioned.

For some days rumours had been circulating that Riordan had been wiped out by the crash. Now his friends rallied to his defence, some with vehement assertions that he never played the market. He had been deeply involved, as subsequent Senate committee investigations of the stock market revealed, but a hurried audit of the bank showed that all of its funds were intact. This fact was well-publicized over the weekend. The City Administration boldly announced that it was leaving its deposits with the bank, which was a trifle like saying that it would remain on speaking terms with Tammany Hall. Raskob temporarily assumed the chairmanship. No run developed. The Church concluded that Riordan, a Catholic, had been temporarily deranged and thus was eligible for burial in consecrated ground. Among the honorary pallbearers were Al Smith, Herbert Lehman, and John J. Raskob, and among those attending the funeral were Mayor Frank Hague, Vincent Astor, Grover Whalen, James A. Farley, and M. J. Meehan, the market operator.

Two and a half years later, on Saturday, 12 March, 1932, Ivar Kreuger shot himself dead in his Paris apartment at eleven o'clock in the morning local time. This was six hours before the New York Stock Exchange closed. With the co-operation of the Paris police, the news was withheld until the market closed. Later a congressional committee was exceedingly critical of this delay, and Al Smith's action was cited in the defence. In the case of Kreuger, it should be added, the security system of the Paris police was less than perfect. It is fairly certain that there was heavy selling that morning – including heavy short selling – of Kreuger and Toll by continental interests.[1]

## 2

In many ways the effect of the crash on embezzlement was more significant than on suicide. To the economist embezzlement is the most interesting of crimes. Alone among the various forms of larceny it has a time parameter. Weeks, months, or years may elapse between the commission of the crime and its discovery. (This is a period, incidentally, when the embezzler has his gain and the man who has been embezzled, oddly enough, feels no loss. There is a net increase in psychic wealth.) At any given time there exists an inventory of undiscovered embezzlement in – or more precisely not in – the country's businesses and banks. This inventory – it should

1. *Stock Exchange Practices*, January 1933, Pt 4, pp. 1214 ff. Such sales were heavy for Friday and Saturday, but in the Exchange records of the time the two days are not segregated. Mr Donald Durant, the highly uninformed American director of Kreuger and Toll, was in Paris at the time of Kreuger's death and cabled the news to the firm of Lee, Higginson and Company, of which he was a partner. The latter company, which was Kreuger's American investment banker, appears to have refrained scrupulously from acting on the news (ibid., pp. 1215–16).

perhaps be called the bezzle – amounts at any moment to many millions of dollars. It also varies in size with the business cycle. In good times people are relaxed, trusting, and money is plentiful. But even though money is plentiful, there are always many people who need more. Under these circumstances the rate of embezzlement grows, the rate of discovery falls off, and the bezzle increases rapidly. In depression all this is reversed. Money is watched with a narrow, suspicious eye. The man who handles it is assumed to be dishonest until he proves himself otherwise. Audits are penetrating and meticulous. Commercial morality is enormously improved. The bezzle shrinks.

The stock market boom and the ensuing crash caused a traumatic exaggeration of these normal relationships. To the normal needs for money, for home, family, and dissipation, was added, during the boom, the new and overwhelming requirements for funds to play the market or to meet margin calls. Money was exceptionally plentiful. People were also exceptionally trusting. A bank president who was himself trusting Kreuger, Hopson, and Insull was obviously unlikely to suspect his lifelong friend the cashier. In the late twenties the bezzle grew apace.

Just as the boom accelerated the rate of growth, so the crash enormously advanced the rate of discovery. Within a few days, something close to universal trust turned into something akin to universal suspicion. Audits were ordered. Strained or preoccupied behaviour was noticed. Most important the collapse in stock values made irredeemable the position of the employee who had embezzled to play the market. He now confessed.

After the first week or so of the crash, reports of defaulting employees were a daily occurrence. They were far more common than the suicides. On some days comparatively brief accounts occupied a column or more in the *Times*. The amounts were large and small, and they were reported from far and wide.

The most spectacular embezzlement of the period – the counterpart of the Riordan suicide – was the looting of the Union Industrial Bank of Flint, Michigan. The gross take, estimates of which grew alarmingly as the investigation proceeded, was stated in *The Literary Digest* later in the year to be $3,592,000.[1]

In the beginning this embezzlement was a matter of individual initiative. Unknown to each other, a number of the bank's officers began making away with funds. Gradually they became aware of each other's activities, and since they could scarcely expose each other, they cooperated. The enterprise eventually embraced about a dozen people, including virtually all of the principal officers of the bank. Operations were so well organized that even the arrival of bank examiners at the local hotels was made known promptly to members of the syndicate.

Most of the funds which were purloined had been deposited with the bank to be loaned in the New York call market. The money was duly dispatched to New York but promptly recalled while the records continued to show that it was there. The money was then returned once more to New York and put into stocks. In the spring of 1929 the group was about $100,000 ahead. Then, unfortunately, it went short just as the market soared into the blue yonder of the summer sky. This was so costly that the group was induced to return to a long position, which it did just before the crash. The crash, needless to say, was mortal.

Each week during the autumn more such unfortunates were revealed in their misery. Most of them were small men who had taken a flier in the market and then become more deeply involved. Later they had more impressive companions. It was

1. 7 December 1929.

the crash, and the subsequent ruthless contraction of values, which, in the end, exposed the speculation by Kreuger, Hopson, and Insull with the money of other people. Should the American economy ever achieve permanent full employment and prosperity, firms should look well to their auditors. One of the uses of depression is the exposure of what auditors fail to find. Bagehot once observed: 'Every great crisis reveals the excessive speculations of many houses which no one before suspected.'[1]

### 3

In mid-November 1929, at long, lost last, the market stopped falling – at least, for a while. The low was on Wednesday, 13 November. On that day the *Times* industrials closed at 224 down from 542, or by almost exactly one-half since 3 September. They were also then down 82 points – about one-quarter – from the close on that day barely two weeks before when John D. Rockefeller had announced that he and his son were buying common stocks. On November 13 there was another Rockefeller story: it was said that the family had entered a million-share buying order to peg Standard Oil of New Jersey at 50. During the rest of November and December the course of the market was moderately up.

The decline had run its course. However, the end coincided with one last effort at reassurance. No one can say for sure that it did no good. One part was the announcement by the New York Stock Exchange of an investigation of short selling. Inevitably in the preceding weeks there had been rumours of bear raids on the market and of fortunes being made by the shorts. The benign people known as 'they', who once had put the market up, were now a malign influence putting it down and making money out of the common disaster. In the early

1. *Lombard Street*, p. 150.

days of the crash it was widely believed that Jesse L. Livermore, a Bostonian with a large and unquestionably exaggerated reputation for bear operations, was heading a syndicate that was driving the market down. So persistent did these rumours become that Livermore, whom few had thought sensitive to public opinion, issued a formal denial that he was involved in any deflationary plot. 'What little business I have done in the stock market', he said, 'has always been as an individual and will continue to be done on such basis.' As early as 24 October, *The Wall Street Journal*, then somewhat less reserved in its view of the world than now, complained that 'there has been a lot of short selling, a lot of forced selling, and a lot of selling to make the market look bad'. Such suspicions the Exchange authorities now sought to dispel. Nothing came of the study.

A more important effort at reassurance was made by President Hoover. Presumably he was still indifferent to the fate of the stock market. But he could not be indifferent to the much-publicized fundamentals, which by now were behaving worse each week. Prices of commodities were falling. Freight-car loadings, pig iron and steel production, coal output, and automobile production were also all going down. So, as a result, was the general index of industrial production. Indeed, it was falling much more rapidly than in the sharp postwar depression of 1920–1. There were alarming stories of the drop in consumer buying, especially of more expensive goods. It was said that sales of radio sets in New York had fallen by half since the crash.

Mr Hoover's first step was out of the later works of John Maynard Keynes. Precisely as Keynes and Keynesians would have advised, he announced a cut in taxes. The rate on both individuals and corporations was cut by one full percentage point. This reduced the income tax of a head of a family with no dependants and an income of $4,000 by two-thirds. The man with $5,000 got a similar reduction. The tax of a married man with no dependants and an income of $10,000 was cut in half. These were dramatic reductions, but their effect was sadly mitigated by the fact that for most people the taxes being cut were already insignificant. The man with $4,000 had his annual tax burden reduced from $5.63 to $1.88. The man with $5,000 got a cut from $16.88 to $5.63. For the man with $10,000 the reduction in annual tax was from $120 to $65. The step, nonetheless, was well received as a contribution to increased purchasing power, expanded business investment, and a general revival of confidence.

Mr Hoover also called a series of meetings on the state of the economy. The leading industrialists, the leading railway executives, the heads of the large utilities, the heads of the important construction companies, the union leaders, and the heads of the farm organizations met in turn with the President during the latter part of November. The procedure in the case of each of the meetings was the same. There was a solemn session with the President, those attending had their picture taken with the President, and there was a press interview at which the conferees gave the press their opinion on the business prospect. The latter, without exception, was highly favourable. After the meeting of the industrial leaders on 21 November, which was attended by, among others, Henry Ford, Walter Teagle, Owen D. Young, Alfred P. Sloan, Jr, Pierre du Pont, Walter Gifford, and Andrew Mellon, the expressions of confidence were so robust that Julius Rosenwald, who also attended, said he feared there might soon be a bad labour shortage.

The utility, rail, and construction executives were equally hopeful. Even the heads of the farm organizations were less misanthropic than normal for that time. They said afterwards that they had told the President that 'the morale of their industry was better than it had been for years'.[1]

1. *Magazine of Wall Street*, 14 December 1929, p. 264. The reference to Foch and the Marne following is from the same source.

was organized reassurance on a really grand scale, and
.tracted some of the most enthusiastic comment of the
.riod. A Wall Street financial writer began his story of the
sessions: '"Order up the Moors!" was Marshal Foch's reply
at the first battle of the Marne . . . "Order up the business
reserves," directed President Hoover as pessimistic reports
flowed in from all quarters following the stock market crash.'
The *Philadelphia Record* was led to describe the President as
'easily the most commanding figure in the modern science of
"engineering statesmanship"'. The *Boston Globe* said that the
nation is now aware 'that it has at the White House a man who
believes not in the philosophy of drift, but in the dynamics of
mastery'.[1]

### 4

Yet to suppose that President Hoover was engaged only in
organizing further reassurance is to do him a serious injustice.
He was also conducting one of the oldest, most important –
and, unhappily, one of the least understood – rites in American
life. This is the rite of the meeting which is called not to do
business but to do no business. It is a rite which is still much
practised in our time. It is worth examining for a moment.

Men meet together for many reasons in the course of business. They need to instruct or persuade each other. They must
agree on a course of action. They find thinking in public
more productive or less painful than thinking in private. But
there are at least as many reasons for meetings to transact no
business. Meetings are held because men seek companionship
or, at a minimum, wish to escape the tedium of solitary duties.
They yearn for the prestige which accrues to the man who
presides over meetings, and this leads them to convoke assem-
blages over which they can preside. Finally, there is the meeting

1. Both comments are from *The Literary Digest*, 30 November 1929.

which is called not because there is business to be done, but because it is necessary to create the impression that business is being done. Such meetings are more than a substitute for action. They are widely regarded as action.

The fact that no business is transacted at a no-business meeting is normally not a serious cause of embarrassment to those attending. Numerous formulas have been devised to prevent discomfort. Thus scholars, who are great devotees of the no-business meeting, rely heavily on the exchange-of-ideas justification. To them the exchange of ideas is an absolute good. Any meeting at which ideas are exchanged is, therefore, useful. This justification is nearly ironclad. It is very hard to have a meeting of which it can be said that no ideas were exchanged.

Salesmen and sales executives, who also are important practitioners of the no-business gathering, commonly have a different justification and one that has strong spiritual overtones. Out of the warmth of comradeship, the interplay of personality, the stimulation of alcohol, and the inspiration of oratory comes an impulsive rededication to the daily task. The meeting pays for itself in a fuller and better life and the sale of more goods in future weeks and months.

The no-business meetings of the great business executives depend for their illusion of importance on something quite different. Not the exchange of ideas or the spiritual rewards of comradeship, but a solemn sense of assembled power gives significance to this assemblage. Even though nothing of importance is said or done, men of importance cannot meet without the occasion seeming important. Even the commonplace observation of the head of a large corporation is still the statement of the head of a large corporation. What it lacks in content it gains in power from the assets behind it.

The no-business meeting was an almost perfect instrument for the situation in which President Hoover found himself in the autumn of 1929. The modest tax cut apart, the President was clearly averse to any large-scale government action to counter the developing depression. Nor was it very certain, at the time, what could be done. Yet by 1929 popular faith in *laissez-faire* had been greatly weakened. No responsible political leader could safely proclaim a policy of keeping hands off. The no-business meetings at the White House were a practical expression of *laissez-faire*. No positive action resulted. At the same time they gave a sense of truly impressive action. The conventions governing the no-business session ensured that there would be no embarrassment arising from the absence of business. Those who attended accepted as a measure of the importance of the meetings the importance of the people attending. The newspapers also cooperated in emphasizing the importance of the sessions. Had they done otherwise they would, of course, have undermined the value of the sessions as news.

In recent times the no-business meeting at the White House – attended by governors, industrialists, representatives of business, labour, and agriculture – has become an established institution of government. Some device for simulating action, when action is impossible, is indispensable in a sound and functioning democracy. Mr Hoover in 1929 was a pioneer in this field of public administration.

As the depression deepened, it was said that Mr Hoover's meetings had been a failure. This, obviously, reflects a very narrow view.

## 5

In January, February, and March of 1930 the stock market showed a substantial recovery. Then in April the recovery lost momentum, and in June there was another large drop. Thereafter, with few exceptions the market dropped week by week, month by month, and year by year through June of 1932. The position when it finally halted made the worst level during the crash seem memorable by contrast. On 13 November 1929, it may be recalled, the *Times* industrials closed at 224. On 8 July 1932, they were 58. This value was not much more than the net by which they dropped on the single day of 28 October 1929. Standard Oil of New Jersey, which the Rockefellers were believed to have pegged at 50 on 13 November 1929, dropped below 20 in April 1932. On 8 July it was 24. U.S. Steel on 8 July reached a low of 22. On 3 September 1929, it had sold as high as 262. General Motors was a bargain at 8 on 8 July, down from 73 on 3 September 1929. Montgomery Ward was 4, down from 138. Tel and Tel was 72, and on 3 September 1929 it had sold at 304. Anaconda sold at 4 on 8 July. *The Commercial and Financial Chronicle* observed that 'the copper shares are so low that their fluctuations are of little consequence'.[1]

However, comparatively speaking, values in these staple stocks had been well maintained. Things were far worse with the investment trusts. Blue Ridge during the week ending 8 July 1932 was 63 cents, and Shenandoah was 50 cents. United Founders and American Founders were both around 50 cents as compared with 70 and 117 (dollars, needless to say) on 3 September 1929. The fears of November 1929 that the investment trusts might go to nothing had been largely realized.

No one any longer suggested that business was sound, fundamentally or otherwise. During the week of 8 July 1932, *Iron Age* announced that steel operations had reached twelve per cent of capacity. This was thought of its sort to be a record. Pig-iron output was the lowest since 1896. A total of 720,278 shares were traded that day on the New York Stock Exchange.

Before all this came to pass there had been more, many

1. 9 July 1932.

more, efforts at reassurance. In the weeks of the crash President Hoover had sagely observed: 'My own experience ... has been that words are not of any great importance in times of economic disturbance.' This impregnable rule he thereafter forgot. In December he told the Congress that the steps he had taken – the White House no-business conferences in particular – had 're-established confidence'. In March 1930, following a flood of optimistic forecasts by his subordinates, Mr Hoover said that the worst effect of the crash upon unemployment would be ended in sixty days. In May Mr Hoover said he was convinced 'we have now passed the worst and with continued unity of effort shall rapidly recover'. Toward the end of the month he said that business would be normal by fall.[1]

What was perhaps the last word on the policy of reassurance was said by Simeon D. Fess, the Chairman of the Republican National Committee:

Persons high in Republican circles are beginning to believe that there is some concerted effort on foot to utilize the stock market as a method of discrediting the Administration. Every time an Administration official gives out an optimistic statement about business conditions, the market immediately drops.[2]

1. Frederick Lewis Allen, *Only Yesterday*, pp. 340–1.
2. Quoted by Edward Angly, *Oh Yeah!*, p. 27, from the *New York World*, 15 October 1930.

# CHAPTER IX

# AFTERMATH II

I

THE crash blighted the fortunes of many hundreds of thousands of Americans. But among people of prominence worse havoc was worked on reputations. In such circles credit for wisdom, foresight, and, unhappily also, for common honesty underwent a convulsive shrinkage.

On the whole, those who had proclaimed during the crash that business was 'fundamentally sound' were not held accountable for their words. The ritualistic nature of their expression was recognized; then as now no one supposed that such spokesmen knew whether business was sound or unsound. One exception was Mr Hoover. He undoubtedly suffered as the result of his repeated predictions of imminent prosperity. However, Hoover had converted the simple business ritual of reassurance into a major instrument of public policy. It was certain in consequence to be the subject of political comment.

The scholarly forecasters were not so fortunate. People on the whole cherished the discovery that they were not omniscient. Mr Lawrence disappeared from Princeton. Among economists his voice was not heard again.

The Harvard Economic Society, it will be recalled, had come up to the summer of the crash with a valuable reputation for pessimism. This position it abandoned during the summer when the stock market kept on rising and business seemed strong. On 2 November, after the crash, the Society concluded that 'the present recession, both for stocks and business, is not the precursor of business depression'. On 10 November it made its notable estimate that 'a serious depression like that of 1920–1 is outside the range of probability'. It repeated this judgement on 23 November and on 21 December gave its forecast for the next year: 'A depression seems improbable; [we expect] recovery of business next spring, with further improvement in the fall.' On 18 January 1930 the Society said, 'There are indications that the severest phase of the recession is over'; on 1 March, that 'manufacturing activity is now – to judge from past periods of contraction – definitely on the road to recovery'; on 22 March, 'The outlook continues favourable'; on 29 March, that 'the outlook is favourable'; on 19 April, that 'by May or June the spring recovery forecast in our letters of last December and November should be clearly apparent'; on 17 May, that business 'will turn for the better this month or next, recover vigorously in the third quarter and end the year at levels substantially above normal'; on 24 May it was suggested that conditions 'continue to justify' the forecasts of 17 May; on 21 June, that 'despite existing irregularities' there would soon be improvement; on 28 June it stated that 'irregular and conflicting movements of business should soon give way to sustained recovery'; on 19 July it pointed out that 'untoward elements have operated to delay recovery but the evidence nonetheless points to substantial improvement'; and on 30 August 1930, the Society stated that 'the present depression has about spent its force'. Thereafter the Society became less hopeful. On 15 November 1930 it said: 'We are now near the end of the declining phase of the depression.' A year later, on 31 October 1931, it said: 'Stabilization at [present] depression levels is clearly possible.'[1] Even these last forecasts were wildly optimistic. Somewhat later, its reputation for infallibility rather dimmed, the Society was dissolved. Harvard economics professors ceased forecasting the future and again donned their accustomed garb of humility.

Professor Irving Fisher tried hard to explain why he had

1. Quotations are from the *Weekly Letters* of the date given.

been wrong. Early in November 1929 he suggested that the whole thing had been irrational and hence beyond prediction. In a statement that was not a model of coherence, he said: 'It was the psychology of panic. It was mob psychology, and it was not, primarily, that the price level of the market was unsoundly high . . . the fall in the market was very largely due to the psychology by which it went down because it went down.'[1] The explanation attracted little attention except from the editor of *The Commercial and Financial Chronicle*. The latter observed with succinct brutality: 'The learned professor is wrong as he usually is when he talks about the stock market.' The 'mob', he added, didn't sell. It got sold out.

Before the year was over, Professor Fisher tried again in a book, *The Stock Market Crash – And After*.[2] He argued, and rightly for the moment, that stocks were still on a plateau, albeit a somewhat lower one than before, that the crash was a great accident, that the market had gone up 'principally because of sound, justified expectations of earnings'. He also argued that prohibition was still a strong force for higher business productivity and profits, and concluded that for 'the immediate future, at least, the outlook is bright'. This book attracted little attention. One trouble with being wrong is that it robs the prophet of his audience when he most needs it to explain why.

Out in Ohio, Professor Dice – he of the parasangs – survived honourably to write and teach for a lifetime about finance.

This may be the place also to record another happy ending. Goldman, Sachs and Company rescued its firm name from its delinquent offspring and returned to an earlier role of strict

1. New York *Herald Tribune*, 3 November 1929. Quoted by *The Commercial and Financial Chronicle*, 9 November 1929.

2. New York (Macmillan), 1930. The quotations following are on pp. 53, 269.

rectitude and stern conservatism. It became known for its business in the most austere of securities.

2

New York's two greatest banks, the Chase and the National City, suffered severely in the aftermath. They, of course, shared the general obloquy of the New York bankers which resulted from the great hopes and great disappointments of organized support. But it was also the remarkable misfortune of each that it had as its head in those days a market operator in the grand manner.

Of the two, the Chase was the more fortunate. Albert H. Wiggin, variously President, Chairman of the board, and Chairman of the governing board of the Chase, was a speculator and operator, but not an articulate one. However, in 1929 and the years preceding he had been engaging in some astonishing enterprises. In 1929 he received $275,000 compensation as head of the Chase. He was also – or while head of the Chase had been – director of some fifty-nine utility, industrial, insurance, and other corporations and from some of these had also received a handsome salary. Armour and Company had paid him $40,000 to be a member of its finance committee; he got $20,000 a year from the Brooklyn-Manhattan Transit Corporation; at least seven other firms paid him from two to five thousand annually.[1] Wisdom and esteem, or even affection, were not the only factors in his compensation. Those who paid were usually clients and prospective borrowers from the Chase. But the most remarkable of Mr Wiggin's extracurricular interests was a bevy of private companies. There were personal holding companies, two of which were named sentimentally for his daughters. Three others were incorporated in Canada for

1. *Stock Exchange Practices*, Report, 1934, p. 201–2.

highly unsentimental reasons of taxation and corporate reticence.[1]

These companies were the instruments for an astonishing variety of stock market operations. In one operation in the spring of 1929 Shermar Corporation – one of the namesake companies – participated with Harry F. Sinclair and Arthur W. Cutten in a mammoth pool in the common stock of Sinclair Consolidated Oil Company. Even in those tolerant days Sinclair and Cutten were considered rather garish companions for a prominent banker. However, the operation netted Shermar $891,600.37 on no apparent investment.[2]

However, the most breathtaking of Mr Wiggin's operations were in the stock of the Chase National Bank. These, in turn, were financed by the Chase bank itself. In one exceptionally well-timed coup Shermar Corporation, between 23 September and 4 November 1929, sold short 42,506 shares of Chase stock. (For those to whom short selling is an unrevealed mystery, this meant in effect that it negotiated a loan of 42,506 shares and then sold them at the exceedingly good prices then obtaining. It did this with the intention of buying the same number of shares later at a lower price in order to repay in kind the lender who had provided the original stock. The profit from repaying shares bought at a lower price – always assuming that the price went down – would obviously accrue to Shermar.) Prices did go down superbly; the short sale anticipated perfectly the crash. Then on 11 December 1929 Murlyn Corporation – this was for another daughter – bought 42,506 shares of stock from an affiliate of the Chase National Bank and financed this purchase with a loan of $6,588,430 from the Chase National Bank and from Shermar Corporation. These shares were used to cover Shermar's short sale, i.e. to repay the loan of securities.

1. *Stock Exchange Practices*, Hearings, October–November 1933, Pt 6, pp. 2877 ff.
2. *Stock Exchange Practices*, Report, 1934, pp. 192–3.

The profits on the operation – at a time when many other people were doing much, much less well – was $4,008,538.[1] People of carping tendencies might hold the profit was earned by the bank, whose stock it was, whose officer Wiggin was, and which had provided the money for the operation. In fact, the gain all went to Wiggin. Mr Wiggin subsequently defended loans by banks to their own officers to allow them to speculate in their own stock on the grounds that it developed an interest in their institution. However, by this line of reasoning, loans to finance short sales present a difficulty: presumably they develop an interest in having the institution, and hence its stock, behave as badly as possible. Pressed on this point, Mr Wiggin expressed doubt as to whether officers should sell their own companies short.

At the end of 1932 Mr Wiggin requested that he not be re-elected Chairman of the Governing Board of the bank. He was approaching sixty-five, and he noted with some slight overstatement that his 'heart and energies [had] been concentrated for many years in promoting the growth, welfare, and usefulness of the Chase National Bank'.[2] It also seems probable that Winthrop W. Aldrich, who had come into the Chase as the result of a merger with the Equitable Trust Company and who represented a more austere tradition in commercial banking – the Equitable was controlled by the Rockefellers – had come to regard Mr Wiggin as dispensable.[3] The Executive Committee of the Chase, 'in order to discharge in some measure the obligations of this bank to Mr Wiggin',[4] by unanimous action voted him a life salary of $100,000. It was later brought out

1. *Stock Exchange Practices*, Report, 1934, pp. 188 ff.

2. *Stock Exchange Practices*, Hearings, October 1933, Pt. 5, p. 2304.

3. Mr Aldrich later told a Senate committee (ibid., p. 4020) that his differences of opinion with friends of Mr Wiggin, and presumably also with Mr Wiggin, were a matter of general knowledge.

4. ibid., p. 2302.

that this gesture of inspired generosity had been the impulse of Mr Wiggin himself. In the months following Mr Wiggin's retirement his activities became a matter of detailed study by a Senate committee, Mr Aldrich, his successor, confessed his surprise at the extent and diversity of his predecessor's enterprises and said that the voting of the life salary was a terrible mistake. Mr Wiggin later renounced the compensation.

### 3

By comparison with the National City the troubles of the Chase were slight. Mr Wiggin was a reserved, some described him as a rather scholarly, man. The head of the National City, Charles E. Mitchell, on the other hand, was a genial extrovert with a talent for headlines. He was known to one and all as a leading prophet of the New Era.

In the autumn of 1929 there were rumours in Wall Street that Mitchell would resign. He did not, and the rumours were described by Percy A. Rockefeller, an associate in numerous rather fervent stock market operations and a director of the bank, as 'too absurd to be considered by any sensible person'.[1] For the next two or three years Mitchell was rather out of the news. Then at nine o'clock on the evening of 21 March 1933 he was arrested by Assistant U.S. District Attorney Thomas E. Dewey and charged with evasion of income taxes.

Many of the facts were never seriously in dispute. Like Wiggin, Mitchell had been operating extensively in the stock of his own bank, although possibly for more defensible reasons. 1929 was a year of bank mergers, and Charles E. Mitchell was no man to resist a trend. By early autumn of 1929 he had all but completed a merger with the Corn Exchange Bank. The directors of the two institutions had approved; all that remained was the formality of ratification

1. *Investment News*, 16 November 1929, p. 546.

by the stockholders. Holders of Corn Exchange stock were to receive, at their option, four-fifths of a share of National City stock or $360 in cash. The price of National City stock was then above 500, so it was certain that the Corn Exchange stockholders would take the stock.

Then came the crash. The price of National City stock dropped to around 425, and at any price below 450 – four-fifths of which equalled $360 in cash – the stockholders of the Corn Exchange would take money. To buy out all the Corn Exchange holders for cash would cost the National City around $200 million. That was too much, so Mitchell undertook to save the deal. He began buying National City stock, and during the week of 28 October he arranged to borrow twelve million dollars from J. P. Morgan and Company with which to buy more. (Twelve million was a sizeable sum both for Mitchell and for Morgan's, even at that time. Only ten million was actually used, and of this four million was repaid within a week or so. Possibly some of the Morgan partners had second thoughts on the wisdom of the loan.)

The coup failed. Like so many others, Mitchell learned how different it was to support a stock when everyone wanted to sell as compared with those days but a few weeks back when everyone wanted to buy. The price of National City stock sank lower and lower. Mitchell reached the end of his resources and gave up. This was no time for false pride, and with some mild prodding from the management, the National City stockholders repudiated that management and rejected the now disastrous deal. Mitchell, however, was left with a formidable debt to J. P. Morgan and Company. This debt was secured by the stock that had been purchased to support the market and by Mitchell's personal holdings, but its value was shrinking grievously. By the end of the year National City stock was near 200, down from more than 500, and close to the value at which Morgan's had accepted it as collateral.

Now Mitchell faced another misfortune, or, rather, an earlier piece of good fortune now became a disaster. As an executive of the National City Bank, Mitchell's pay was a modest $25,000. However, the bank had an incentive system which may still hold some sort of record for munificence. After a deduction of eight per cent, twenty per cent of the profits of the bank, and of its security affiliate, the National City Company were paid into a management fund. This was divided twice a year between the principal officers by an arrangement which must have made for an interesting half-hour. Each officer first dropped in a hat an unsigned ballot suggesting the share of the fund that Chairman Mitchell should have. Then each signed a ballot giving his estimate of the worth of each of the other eligible officers, himself excluded. The average of these estimates guided the Executive Committee of the bank in fixing the percentages of the fund each officer was to have.

The years 1928 and 1929 were a time of excellent profits. Mitchell's subordinates had also taken a favourable view of his work. For the full year 1928 his cut was $1,316,634.14. 1929 was even better. The division at the end of the first half of that year brought him no less than $1,108,000.[1] Dividends and numerous other activities had further augmented his income, and all of this meant a serious tax liability. It would have been easy to sell some National City stock and establish a tax loss, but, as noted, the stock was pledged with J. P. Morgan and Company.

Nevertheless, Mitchell sold the stock – to his wife: 18,300 shares were disposed of to this possibly unsuspecting lady at 212, for the exceedingly satisfying loss of $2,872,305.50. This wiped out all tax liability for 1929. Morgan's were not, it appears, notified of the change of ownership of the stock they held. Somewhat later Mitchell reacquired the stock from his wife, also at a price of 212. Before then there had been a

1. *Stock Exchange Practices*, Report, 1934, p. 206.

further sickening slide in the price, and had Chairman Mitchell bought the stock in the open market rather than from his wife, he could have got it for around 40. Asked about the transaction by Senator Brookhard of Iowa during a Senate hearing, Mitchell, in a burst of candour that must have devastated his lawyer, said: 'I sold this stock, frankly, for tax purposes.'[1] This frankness led directly to his indictment a few weeks later.

Following his testimony, Mitchell had resigned from the National City Bank. His trial in New York during May and June of 1933 was something of a sensation, although the head-lines were necessarily subordinate to the larger ones currently being made in Washington. In his inaugural address on 4 March, Roosevelt had promised to drive the money-changers from the temple. Mitchell was widely regarded as the first.

On 22 June, Mitchell was acquitted by the jury on all counts. The sales as required by the tax laws were held to be bona fide transactions made in good faith. The *Times* reporter covering the trial thought that both Mitchell and his lawyer received the verdict with surprise. Attorney General Cummings said that he still believed in the jury system. Mitchell later resumed his career in Wall Street as head of Blyth and Company. The government entered a civil claim for taxes and won a judgement of $1,100,000 in taxes and penalties. Mitchell appealed the case through to the Supreme Court, lost, and made a final settlement with the government on 27 December 1938. On his behalf it must be stressed that the device by which he sought to reduce his tax liability was far more common then than now. The Senate investigations of 1933 and 1934 showed that tax avoidance had brought individuals of the highest respectability into extraordinary financial intercourse with their wives.[2]

1. *Stock Exchange Practices*, Report, 1934, p. 322.
2. ibid., pp. 321, 322.

4

Our political tradition sets great store by the generalized symbol of evil. This is the wrongdoer whose wrongdoing will be taken by the public to be the secret propensity of a whole community or class. We search avidly for such people, not so much because we wish to see them exposed and punished as individuals, but because we cherish the resulting political discomfort of their friends. To uncover an evil man among the friend of one's foes has long been a recognized method of advancing one's political fortunes. However, in recent times the technique has been greatly improved and refined by the added firmness with which the evil of the evildoer is now attributed to friends, acquaintances, and all who share his way of life.

In the nineteen-thirties Wall Street was exceptionally well endowed with enemies. There were some socialists and communists who believed that capitalism should be abolished and obviously did not seek to have its citadel preserved. There were some people who merely thought that Wall Street was bad. There were yet others who did not seek to have Wall Street abolished or who did not care much about its allegedly evil ways but who enjoyed as a matter of course the discomfiture of the rich and the powerful and the proud. There were those who had lost money in Wall Street. Most of all there was the New Deal. The administrations of Coolidge and Hoover had had an extremely overt alliance with the great financial interests which Wall Street symbolized. With the advent of the New Deal the sins of Wall Street became the sins of the political enemy. What was bad for Wall Street was bad for the Republican Party.

For anyone who was in search of symbolic evil in Wall Street – of individuals whose misbehaviour would stigmatize the whole community – the discovery that the heads of the

National City and Chase had been guilty of grave lapses would seem to be almost ideal. These were the two best known and most influential banks; what could have been better than default here?

That the shortcomings of Mr Wiggin and Mr Mitchell were much welcomed is, of course, clear. Yet in some indefinable sense they were not of that part of Wall Steet that people suspected most. Wall Street's crime, in the eyes of its classic enemies, was less its power than its morals. And the centre of immorality was not the banks but the stock market. It was on the stock market that men gambled not alone with their own money, but with the wealth of the country. The stock market, with its promise of easy riches, was what led good if not very wise men to perdition – like the cashier of the local bank who was also a vestryman. The senseless gyrations of the stock market affected farm prices and land values and the renewal of notes and mortgages. Though to the sophisticated radical the banks might be the real menace, sound populist attitudes pointed the finger of suspicion at the New York Stock Exchange. There, accordingly, was the place, if possible, to find the symbol of evil, for there was the institution about which people were ready to believe the worst.

The search for a really adequate miscreant in the Stock Exchange began in April 1932. The task was undertaken by the Senate Committee on Banking and Currency (later by a subcommittee) and its instructions, graced by the usual split infinitive, were 'to thoroughly investigate practices of stock exchanges . . .' Under the later guidance of Ferdinand Pecora, this committee became the scourge of commercial, investment, and private bankers. But this was not foreseen when it was organized. The original and more or less exclusive object of the inquiry was the market for securities.

On the whole, this part of the investigation was unproductive. The first witness, when the hearings opened on 11 April

1932, was Richard Whitney.[1] On 30 November 1929, the
Governing Committee of the New York Stock Exchange had
passed a resolution of appreciation for the 'efficient and con-
scientious' labours of their acting president during the recent
storm. It is an 'old saying', the Resolution had stated, 'that
great emergencies produce the men who are competent to deal
with them . . .' This sense of indebtedness made it inevitable
that when Edward H. H. Simmons retired as President of the
Exchange in 1930 after six years in office, Whitney would be
elected to succeed him. As President of the Exchange it thus
fell to Whitney, in the spring of 1932, to assume the task of
protecting the stock market from its critics.

Whitney was not in all respects an ingratiating witness. One
of his successors in office not long ago compared his general
manner and bearing with that of Secretary of Defence Charles
E. Wilson at the hearings on his confirmation as Secretary of
Defence in early 1953. Whitney admitted to no serious fault
in the past operations of the Exchange or even to the possibility
of error. He supplied the information that was requested, but
he was not unduly helpful to senators who sought to penetrate
the mysteries of short selling, sales against the box, options,
pools, and syndicates. He seemed to feel that these things
were beyond the senators' intelligence. Alternatively he implied
that they were things that every intelligent schoolboy understood and it was painful for him to have to go over the obvious.
He was so unwise as to get into a discussion of personal economic philosophy with Senator Smith W. Brookhart of Iowa,
one of the committee members who believed, devoutly, that
the Exchange was the particular invention of the devil. The
government, not Wall Street, was responsible for the current
bad times, Whitney averred, and the government, he believed,
could make its greatest contribution to recovery by balancing
the budget and thus restoring confidence. To balance the

1. *Stock Exchange Practices*, Hearings, April 1932, Pt 1, pp. 1 ff.

budget he recommended cutting the pensions and benefits of veterans who had no service-connected disability and also all government salaries. When asked about cutting his own pay he said no – it was 'very little'. Pressed for the amount, he said that currently it was only about $60,000. His attention was drawn by the committee members to the fact that this was six times what a senator received, but Whitney remained adamantly in favour of cutting the public pay, including that of senators.[1]

In spite of Whitney's manner, or possibly because of it, several days of questioning produced little evidence of wrong-doing and no identification of wrongdoers. Prior to the crash Whitney had heard generally of syndicates and pools, but he could give no details. He repeatedly assured the committee that the Exchange had these and other matters well under control. He took exception to Senator Brookhart's contention that the market was a gambling hell and should be padlocked. In the end Whitney was excused before he had quite completed his testimony.

When the interrogation of Whitney showed clear signs of being unproductive, the committee turned to the famous market operators. These, too, were disappointing. All that could be proved was what everyone knew, namely, that Bernard E. ('Sell 'em Ben') Smith, M. J. Meehan, Arthur W. Cutten, Harry F. Sinclair, Percy A. Rockefeller, and others had been engaged in large-scale efforts to rig the market. Harry F. Sinclair, for example, was shown to have engaged in especially extensive operations in Sinclair Consolidated Oil. This was much like identifying William Z. Foster with the Communist Party. It was impossible to imagine Harry Sinclair not being involved in some intricate manoeuvre in high finance. Moreover, reprehensible as these activities were, it remained that only three short years before they had been

1. *Stock Exchange Practices*, Hearings, February–March 1933, Pt 6, pp. 2235 ff.

regarded with breathless admiration. The problem here was somewhat similar to that encountered in the great red-hunt of the latter forties. Then there was constant embarrassment over the short time that had elapsed since Red Russia had been our gallant Soviet ally.

It is true that the big operators, as they appeared on the stand, were not an especially prepossessing group. As noted earlier, Arthur Cutten's memory was extremely defective. M. J. Meehan was in bad health and mistakenly went abroad when he was supposed to go to Washington. (He later apologized handsomely for the error.) Few of the others could remember much about their operations, Napoleonic though they had once seemed. But men cannot be brought to trial for being unprepossessing. And the dubious demeanour and bad memories of the market operators did not directly involve the reputation of the New York Stock Exchange. It is possible to have a poor view of touts, tipsters, and bookies without thinking the worse of Churchill Downs.

In earlier times of trouble on the stock market, Stock Exchange firms had failed, on occasion by the score. In the fall of 1929 the failures were unimportant. In the first week of the crash no member firm of the New York Stock Exchange had to suspend; only one smallish member firm went under during the period of panic. There were some complaints by customers of mistreatment. But there were more customers who, during the worst days, were carried by their brokers after their margins had been impaired or depleted. The standards of commercial morality of the members of the Exchange would seem to have been well up to the average of the late twenties. They may have been much more rigorous. This would seem to be the most obvious explanation why the Exchange and its members survived so well the investigations of the thirties. They did not come through unscathed, but they suffered no obloquy comparable, say, with that of the great

bankers. In the congressional investigations no flagrant miscreant of any kind was uncovered on the Exchange to serve as
the symbolic bad apple. Then, on 10 March 1938, District
Atttorney Thomas E. Dewey – who had arrested Charles E.
Mitchell and who somehow has escaped a reputation as the
nemesis of Wall Street – ordered the arraignment of Richard
Whitney. The charge was grand larceny.

## 5

The rush to get in on the act, to use the recent idiom, when
Whitney was arrested is a measure of the yearning for a male-
factor in the stock market. It can be compared only with the
stampede which followed the announcement by Attorney
General Herbert Brownell in the autumn of 1953 that former
President Truman had shielded treason. On the day following
his first arrest, Whitney was arrested again by New York State
Attorney General John J. Bennett. Mr Bennett had been conducting an investigation of Whitney's affairs, and he bitterly
accused Mr Dewey of legal claim-jumping. In the next few weeks
virtually every public body or tribunal with a plausible excuse
for doing so, called Whitney to enlarge on his wrongdoing.

The detailed story of Richard Whitney's misfortunes does not
belong to this chronicle. Many of them occurred after the
period with which this history is concerned. There is need here
to cover only those operations that were deemed to implicate
the market.

Whitney's dishonesty was of a casual, rather juvenile sort.
Associates of the day have since explained it as the result of an
unfortunate failure to realize that the rules, which were meant
for other people, also applied to him. Much more striking
than Whitney's dishonesty was the clear fact that he was one of
the most disastrous businessmen in modern history. Theft was
almost a minor incident pertaining to his business misfortunes.

In the twenties the Wall Street firm of Richard Whitney and Company was an unspectacular bond house with a modest business. Whitney apparently felt that it provided insufficient scope for his imagination, and with the passing years he moved on to other enterprises, including the mining of mineral colloids and the marketing of peat humus in Florida. He had also become interested in the distilling of alcoholic beverages, mainly applejack, in New Jersey. Nothing is so voracious as a losing business, and eventually Whitney had three of them. To keep them going he borrowed from banks, investment bankers, other Stock Exchange members, and heavily from his brother, George Whitney, a partner of J. P. Morgan and Company. The loans so negotiated, from the early twenties on, totalled in the millions, many of them unsecured. As time passed Whitney was increasingly pressed. When one loan became due he was forced to replace it with another and to borrow still more for the interest on those outstanding. Beginning in 1933 his Stock Exchange firm was insolvent, although this did not become evident for some five years.[1]

Finally, like so many others, Richard Whitney learned the cost of supporting a stock on a falling market. In 1933, Richard Whitney and Company – the affairs of Whitney and his company were almost completely indistinguishable – had invested in between ten and fifteen thousand shares of Distilled Liquors Corporation, the New Jersey manufacturer of applejack and other intoxicants. The price was $15 a share. In the spring of 1934 the stock reached 45 in over-the-counter trading. In January 1935 it was listed on the New York Curb Exchange. Inevitably Whitney posted the stock as collateral for various of his loans.

Unhappily, popular enthusiasm for the products of the firm,

1. These details are from *Securities and Exchange Commission in the Matters of Richard Whitney, Edwin D. Morgan, Etc.*, Vol. I, Report on Investigation, Washington, 1938.

even in the undiscriminating days following repeal, was remarkably slight. The firm made no money and by June 1936 the price of the stock was down to 11. This drop had a disastrous effect on its value as collateral, and the unhappy Whitney tried to maintain the value by buying more of it. (He later made the claim that he wanted to provide the other investors in the company with a market for their stock,[1] which if true meant that he was engaging in one of the most selfless acts since the death of Sydney Carton.) All the other investors unloaded on Whitney. At the time of his failure, of the 148,750 shares outstanding, Whitney or his firm owned 137,672. By then the value had dropped to between three and four dollars a share. Mention has been made of the tendency of people in this period to swindle themselves. Whitney, in his effort to support the stock of Distilled Liquors Corporation, unquestionably emerged as the Ponzi of financial self-deception. As the result of his operation he had all his old debts, many new ones incurred in supporting the stock, all the stock – and the stock was nearly worthless.

As his position became more complex, Richard Whitney resorted increasingly to an expedient which he had been using for several years – that of posting securities belonging to other people which were in his custody as collateral for his loans. By early 1938 he had reached the end of a surprising capacity to borrow money. Late in the preceding autumn he had had a large last loan from his brother to release securities belonging to the gratuity fund of the Stock Exchange – a fund out of which payments were made on the death of members – which he had appropriated and pledged for a bank loan. He was now desperately, almost pathetically, visiting the most casual of acquaintances in search of funds. The rumour spread that he was in poor condition. Still, on 8 March, there was a stunned silence on the floor of the Exchange when President Charles R. Gay announced from the rostrum the suspension of Richard Whitney

1. *Securities and Exchange Commission*, op. cit., Vol. II. p. 50.

and Company for insolvency. Members were rather more aghast when they learned that Whitney had been engaged in theft on a large scale for a long period.

With no small dignity Whitney made a full disclosure of his operations, refused to enter any sort of plea in his own defence, and passed permanently from sight.

6

The failure of the smallest country banker caused more personal hardship, anguish, and privation than the insolvency of Richard Whitney. His victims were almost uniquely able to afford their loss. And the sums which he stole, while substantial, did not place him in the ranks of the great defaulters of the day – they would not have paid the interest on Ivar Kreuger's larceny for a year. Yet, from the point of view of the antagonists of Wall Street, his default was ideal. Rarely has a crime been more joyously received.

Whitney's identification was wholly with the Stock Exchange, the symbolic centre of sin. Moreover, he had been its president and its uncompromising defender before the Congress and the public in its period of trial. He was a Republican, an arch-conservative, and was loosely associated in the financial community with J. P. Morgan and Company. He had himself taken a strong position in favour of honesty. Speaking in St Louis in 1932, at a time when his own larceny was already well advanced, Whitney had said sternly that one of the prime necessities 'of a great market is that brokers must be honest and financially responsible'. He looked forward to the day when the financial supervision by the Exchange of its members would be so strict that failure 'will be next to impossible'.[1]

1. *The New York Stock Exchange*, an address by Richard Whitney before the Industrial Club of St Louis and the Chamber of Commerce of St Louis (St Louis, 27 September 1932).

Finally, even by his colleagues, Whitney was regarded as a trifle upstage. In his last days he had been reduced to the ultimate indignity of trying to borrow money from the market operator, Bernard E. Smith. Smith, at best a lower middle-brow figure, later told a Securities and Exchange Commission examiner: 'He came up to see me and said he would like to get this over quickly, and told me he would like to borrow $250,000 on his face. I remarked he was putting a pretty high value on his face, so he said . . . his back was to the wall and he had to have $250,000. I told him he had a lot of nerve to ask me for $250,000 when he didn't even bid me the time of day. I told him I frankly didn't like him – that I wouldn't loan him a dime.'[1] On any free vote for the man best qualified to bring discredit to Wall Street, Whitney would have won by a wide margin.

The parallel between Whitney and a more recent culprit is interesting. During the thirties the New Dealers were exuberantly uncovering the financial derelictions of their opposition. (It is interesting that dishonesty and not the more orthodox offences of capitalism like abuse of power or the exploitation of the people was in these days the nemesis of conservatives.) In the nineteen-forties and fifties Republicans, as avidly, were discovering that there were New Dealers who had been communists. Thus it came about that a decade later the counterpart of Richard Whitney was Alger Hiss.

Each served admirably the enemies of his class. Each in origin, education, associations, and career pretensions epitomized that class. In each case the first reaction of friends to the allegations of guilt was disbelief. Whitney's past role in his community had been more prominent, and hence from the viewpoint of his enemies he was a more satisfactory figure than Alger Hiss. In the government hierarchy, Hiss was a distinctly

1. *Securities and Exchange Commission*, op. cit., Transcript of Hearings, Vol. II, pp. 822, 823.

routine figure. His eminence as a global statesman was syn-thesized *ex post facto* and he also gained much prominence during two long trials. Whitney, with no fanfare, accepted his fate.

There is, perhaps, a moral worth drawing from the careers of Whitney and Hiss. Neither the fact that Whitney was con-victed of purloining securities nor that Hiss purloined docu-ments is convincing proof that their friends, associates, and contemporaries were doing the same. On the contrary, the evidence would indicate that most brokers were honest as a matter of absolute routine, and most New Dealers, so far from being in league with the Russians, wished only that they might be invited once to taste caviare at the Soviet embassy. Both liberals and conservatives, left and right, have now had personal experience with the use of the symbolic evil. The injustice of the device is evident. What may be a more compelling point, so are its dangers. In accordance with an old but not outworn tradition, it might now be wise for all to conclude that crime, or even misbehaviour, is the act of an individual, not the pre-disposition of a class.

## 7

The Whitney affair brought a marked change in the relations between the Exchange and the federal government, and, in some measure, between the Exchange and the general public. In the Securities Act of 1933, and more comprehensively in the Securities Exchange Act of 1934, the government had sought to prohibit some of the more spectacular extravagances of 1928 and 1929. Full disclosure was required on new security issues, although no way was found of making would-be investors read what was disclosed. Inside operations and short selling after the manner of Mr Wiggin were outlawed. Authority was given to the Federal Reserve Board to fix margin requirements and these could, if necessary, be made a hundred per cent and thus eliminate margin trading entirely. Pool operations, wash sales, the dissemination of tips or patently false information and other devices for rigging or manipulating the market were prohibited. Commercial banks were divorced from their securities affiliates. Most important, the principle was enunciated that the New York Stock Exchange and the other exchanges were subject to public regulation and the Securities and Exchange Commission was established to apply and enforce such regulation.

This was somewhat bitter medicine. Moreover, regulatory bodies, like the people who comprise them, have a marked life cycle. In youth they are vigorous, aggressive, evangelistic, and even intolerant. Later they mellow, and in old age – after a matter of ten or fifteen years – they become, with some exceptions, either an arm of the industry they are regulating or senile. The S.E.C. was especially aggressive. To any young regulatory body, after all, Wall Street was certain to seem a challenging antagonist.

Until the Whitney affair Wall Street – always with exceptions – was disposed to fight back. It insisted on the right of a financial community in general, and of a securities market in particular, to conduct its affairs in its own way, by its own light and to govern itself. On the evening before the suspension of Whitney was announced from the rostrum, Charles R. Gay, President of the Exchange, and Howland S. Davis, Chairman of the Committee on Business Conduct – Whitney had been a predecessor of both in the two offices – made their way to Washington. There they reported their unhappy news to William O. Douglas and John W. Hanes of the S.E.C. The trip, in far more than a symbolic sense, represented the surrender of the Exchange. The cold war over regulation came to an end and was not thereafter resumed.

While the Whitney default confirmed the victory of the New Deal on the issue of regulation and also served admirably to confirm the more general suspicion of moral delinquency in downtown New York, it was Wall Street's good fortune that it came late. By 1938 the New Deal assault on big business was on the wane; some leaders of the original shock troops were already polishing up speeches on the virtues of the free enterprise system. By then, also, it was accepted New Deal theology that all necessary economic reforms had been revealed and those that had not been enacted were on request from Congress. No further reforms of the securities markets of any importance were on the agenda. Henceforth Wall Street looked ingratiatingly at Washington and Washington merely looked blank.

# CHAPTER X

# CAUSE AND CONSEQUENCE

## I

AFTER the Great Crash came the Great Depression which lasted, with varying severity, for ten years. In 1933, Gross National Product (total production of the economy) was nearly a third less than in 1929. Not until 1937 did the physical volume of production recover to the levels of 1929, and then it promptly slipped back again. Until 1941 the dollar value of production remained below 1929. Between 1930 and 1940 only once, in 1937, did the average number unemployed during the year drop below eight million. In 1933 nearly thirteen million were out of work, or about one in every four in the labour force. In 1938 one person in five was still out of work.[1]

It was during this dreary time that 1929 became a year of myth. People hoped that the country might get back to twenty-nine; in some industries or towns when business was phenomenally good it was almost as good as in twenty-nine; men of outstanding vision, on occasions of exceptional solemnity, were heard to say that 1929 'was no better than Americans deserve'.

On the whole, the great stock market crash can be much more readily explained than the depression that followed it. And among the problems involved in assessing the causes of depression none is more intractable than the responsibility to be assigned to the stock market crash. Economics still does not allow final answers on these matters. But, as usual, something can be said.

1. *Economic Indicators: Historical and Descriptive Supplement*, Joint Committee on the Economic Report, Washington, 1953.

2

As already so often emphasized, the collapse in the stock market in the autumn of 1929 was implicit in the speculation that went before. The only question concerning that speculation was how long it would last. Sometime, sooner or later, confidence in the short-run reality of increasing common stock values would weaken. When this happened, some people would sell, and this would destroy the reality of increasing values. Holding for an increase would now become meaningless; the new reality would be falling prices. There would be a rush, pellmell, to unload. This was the way past speculative orgies had ended. It was the way the end came in 1929. It is the way speculation will end in the future.

We do not know why a great speculative orgy occurred in 1928 and 1929. The long-accepted explanation that credit was easy and so people were impelled to borrow money to buy common stock on margin is obviously nonsense. On numerous occasions before and since credit has been easy, and there has been no speculation whatever. Furthermore, much of the 1928 and 1929 speculation occurred on money borrowed at interest rates which for years before, and in any period since, would have been considered exceptionally astringent. Money, by the ordinary tests, was tight in the late twenties.

Far more important than rate of interest and the supply of credit is the mood. Speculation on a large scale requires a pervasive sense of confidence and optimism and conviction that ordinary people were meant to be rich. People must also have faith in the good intentions and even in the benevolence of others, for it is by the agency of others that they will get rich. In 1929 Professor Dice observed: 'The common folks believe in their leaders. We no longer look upon the captains of industry as magnified crooks. Have we not heard their voices over the radio? Are we not familiar with their thoughts, ambitions, and ideals as they have expressed them to us almost as a man talks to his friend?'[1] Such a feeling of trust is essential for a boom. When people are cautious, questioning, misanthropic, suspicious, or mean, they are immune to speculative enthusiasms.

Savings must also be plentiful. Speculation, however it may rely on borrowed funds, must be nourished in part by those who participate. If savings are growing rapidly, people will place a lower marginal value on their accumulation; they will be willing to risk some of it against the prospect of a greatly enhanced return. Speculation, accordingly, is most likely to break out after a substantial period of prosperity, rather than in the early phases of recovery from a depression. Macaulay noted that between the Restoration and the Glorious Revolution Englishmen were at loss to know what to do with their savings and that the 'natural effect of this state of things was that a crowd of projectors, ingenious and absurd, honest and knavish, employed themselves in devising new schemes for the employment of redundant capital'. Bagehot and others have attributed the South Sea Bubble to roughly the same causes.[2] In 1720 England had enjoyed a long period of prosperity, enhanced in part by war expenditures, and during this time private savings are believed to have grown at an unprecedented rate. Investment outlets were also few and returns low. Accordingly, Englishmen were anxious to place their savings at the disposal of the new enterprises and were quick to believe that the prospects were not fantastic. So it was in 1928 and 1929.

Finally, a speculative outbreak has a greater or less immunizing effect. The ensuing collapse automatically destroys the very mood speculation requires. It follows that an outbreak of speculation provides a reasonable assurance that another out-

1. *New Levels in the Stock Market*, p. 257.
2. Walter Bagehot, *Lombard Street*, p. 130. The quotation from Macaulay, above, is cited by Bagehot, p. 128.

break will not immediately occur. With time and the dimming of memory, the immunity wears off. A recurrence becomes possible. Nothing would have induced Americans to launch a speculative adventure in the stock market in 1935. By 1955 the chances are very much better.

### 3

As noted, it is easier to account for the boom and crash in the market than to explain their bearing on the depression which followed. The causes of the Great Depression are still far from certain. A lack of certainty, it may also be observed, is not evident in the contemporary writing on the subject. Much of it tells what went wrong and why with marked firmness. However, this paradoxically can itself be an indication of uncertainty. When people are least sure they are often most dogmatic. We do not know what the Russians intend, so we state with great assurance what they will do. We compensate for our inability to foretell the consequences of, say rearming Germany by asserting positively just what the consequences will be. So it is in economics. Yet, in explaining what happened in 1929 and after, one can distinguish between explanations that might be right and those that are clearly wrong.

A great many people have always felt that a depression was inevitable in the thirties. There had been (at least) seven good years; now by occult or biblical law of compensation there would have to be seven bad ones. Perhaps, consciously or unconsciously, an argument that was valid for the stock market was brought to bear on the economy in general. Because the market took leave of reality in 1928 and 1929, it had at some time to make a return to reality. The disenchantment was bound to be as painful as the illusions were beguiling. Similarly, the New Era prosperity would some day evaporate; in its wake would come the compensating hardship.

There is also the slightly more subtle conviction that economic life is governed by an inevitable rhythm. After a certain time prosperity destroys itself and depression corrects itself. In 1929 prosperity, in accordance with the dictates of the business cycle, had run its course. This was the faith confessed by the members of the Harvard Economic Society in the spring of 1929 when they concluded that a recession was somehow overdue.

Neither of these beliefs can be seriously supported. The twenties by being comparatively prosperous established no imperative that the thirties be depressed. In the past, good times have given way to less good times and less good or bad to good. But change is normal in a capitalist economy. The degree of regularity in such movements is not great, though often thought to be.[1] No inevitable rhythm required the collapse and stagnation of 1930–40.

Nor was the economy of the United States in 1929 subject to such physical pressure or strain as the result of its past level of performance that a depression was bound to come. The notion that the economy requires occasional rest and resuscitation has a measure of plausibility and also a marked viability. During the summer of 1954 a professional economist on President Eisenhower's personal staff explained the then current recession by saying that the economy was enjoying a brief (and presumably well-merited) rest after the exceptional exertions of preceding years. In 1929 the labour force was not tired; it could have continued to produce indefinitely at the best 1929 rate. The capital plant of the country was not depleted. In the preceding years of prosperity, plant had been renewed and improved. In fact, depletion of the capital plant

1. 'At present it is less likely that the existence of business cycles will be denied than that their regularity will be exaggerated.' Wesley Clair Mitchell, *Business Cycles and Unemployment*, New York (McGraw-Hill), 1923, p. 6.

occurred during the ensuing years of idleness when new investment was sharply curtailed. Raw materials in 1929 were ample for the current rate of production. Entrepreneurs were never more eupeptic. Obviously if men, materials, plant, and management were all capable of continued and even enlarged exertions a refreshing pause was not necessary.

Finally, the high production of the twenties did not, as some have suggested, outrun the wants of the people. During these years people were indeed being supplied with an increasing volume of goods. But there is no evidence that their desire for automobiles, clothing, travel, recreation, or even food was sated. On the contrary, all subsequent evidence showed (given the income to spend) a capacity for a large further increase in consumption. A depression was not needed so that people's wants could catch up with their capacity to produce.

4

What, then, are the plausible causes of the depression? The task of answering can be simplified somewhat by dividing the problem into two parts. First there is the question of why economic activity turned down in 1929. Second there is the vastly more important question of why, having started down, on this unhappy occasion it went down and down and down and remained low for a full decade.

As noted, the Federal Reserve indexes of industrial activity and of factory production, the most comprehensive monthly measures of economic activity then available, reached a peak in June. They then turned down and continued to decline throughout the rest of the year. The turning point in other indicators – factory payrolls, freight-car loadings, and department store sales – came later, and it was October or after before the trend in all of them was clearly down. Still, as economists have generally insisted, and the matter has the high authority of the

National Bureau of Economic Research,[1] the economy had weakened in the early summer well before the crash.

This weakening can be variously explained. Production of industrial products, for the moment, had outrun consumer and investment demand for them. The most likely reason is that business concerns, in the characteristic enthusiasm of good times, misjudged the prospective increase in demand and acquired larger inventories than they later found they needed. As a result they curtailed their buying, and this led to a cutback in production. In short, the summer of 1929 marked the beginning of the familiar inventory recession. The proof is not conclusive from the (by present standards) limited figures available. Department store inventories, for which figures are available, seem not to have been out of line early in the year. But a mild slump in department store sales in April could have been a signal for curtailment.

Also there is a chance – one that students of the period have generally favoured – that more deep-seated factors were at work and made themselves seriously evident for the first time during that summer. Throughout the twenties production and productivity per worker grew steadily: between 1919 and 1929, output per worker in manufacturing industries increased by about forty-three per cent.[2] Wages, salaries, and prices all remained comparatively stable, or in any case underwent no comparable increase. Accordingly, costs fell and with prices the same, profits increased. These profits sustained the spending of the well-to-do, and they also nourished at least some of the expectations behind the stock market boom. Most of all they encouraged a very high level of capital investment. During

1. Geoffrey H. Moore, *Statistical Indications of Cyclical Revivals and Recessions, Occasional Paper 31*, National Bureau of Economic Research, Inc., New York, 1950.

2. H. W. Arndt, *The Economic Lessons of the Nineteen-Thirties*, London (Oxford), 1944, p. 15.

the twenties, the production of capital goods increased at an average annual rate of 6.4 per cent a year; non-durable consumers' goods, a category which includes such objects of mass consumption as food and clothing, increased at a rate of only 2.8 per cent.[1] (The rate of increase for durable consumers' goods such as cars, dwellings, home furnishings, and the like, much of it representing expenditures of the well-off to well-to-do, was 5.9 per cent.) A large and increasing investment in capital goods was, in other words, a principal device by which the profits were being spent.[2] It follows that anything that interrupted the investment outlays – anything, indeed, which kept them from showing the necessary rate of increase – could cause trouble. When this occurred, compensation through an increase in consumer spending could not automatically be expected. The effect, therefore, of insufficient investment – investment that failed to keep pace with the steady increase in profits – could be falling total demand reflected in turn in falling orders and output. Again there is no final proof of this point, for unfortunately we do not know how rapidly investment had to grow to keep abreast of the current increase in profits.[3] However, the explanation is broadly consistent with the facts.

1. E. M. Hugh-Jones and E. A. Radice, *An American Experiment*, London (Oxford), 1936, p. 49. Cited by Arndt, op. cit., p. 16.

2. This has been widely noted. See Lionel Robbins, *The Great Depression*, p. 4, and Thomas Wilson, *Fluctuations in Income*, pp. 154 ff., and J. M. Keynes, *A Treatise on Money*, New York (Harcourt, Brace), 1930, II, 190 ff.

3. Perhaps I may be permitted to enlarge on this in slightly more technical terms. The interruption could as well have been caused by an insufficient rate of increase in consumer spending as by a failure in the greater rate of increase of capital goods spending. Under-consumption and under-investment are the same side of the same coin. And some force is added to this explanation by the fact that spending for one important consumers' durable, namely houses, had been declining for several years and suffered a further substantial drop in 1929. However, the investment function we still suppose to be less

There are other possible explanations of the downturn. Behind the insufficient advance in investment may have been the high interest rates. Perhaps, although less probably, trouble was transmitted to the economy as a whole from some weak sector like agriculture. Further explanations could be offered. But one thing about this experience is clear. Until well along in the autumn of 1929 the downturn was limited. The recession in business activity was modest and under-employment relatively slight. Up to November it was possible to argue that not much of anything had happened. On other occasions, as noted – in 1924 and 1927 and of late in 1949 – the economy has undergone similar recession. But, unlike these other occasions, in 1929 the recession continued and continued and got violently worse. This is the unique feature of the 1929 experience. This is what we need really to understand.

## 5

There seems little question that in 1929, modifying a famous cliché, the economy was fundamentally unsound. This is a circumstance of first-rate importance. Many things were wrong, but five weaknesses seem to have had an especially intimate bearing on the ensuing disaster. They are:

(1) The bad distribution of income. In 1929 the rich were indubitably rich. The figures are not entirely satisfactory, but

---

stable than the consumption function, even though we are less assured of the stability of the latter than we used to be. And in the present case it seems wise to attach causal significance to the part of the spending which had to maintain the largest rate of increase if total spending were to be uninterrupted. The need to maintain a specific rate of increase in investment outlay is insufficiently emphasized by Mr Thomas Wilson in his book which I have so frequently cited and to which students of the period are indebted.

it seems certain that the five per cent of the population with the highest incomes in that year received approximately one-third of all personal income. The proportion of personal income received in the form of interest, dividends, and rent – the income, broadly speaking, of the well-to-do – was about twice as great as in the years following the Second World War.[1]

This highly unequal income distribution meant that the economy was dependent on a high level of investment or a high level of luxury consumer spending or both. The rich cannot buy great quantities of bread. If they are to dispose of what they receive it must be on luxuries or by way of investment in new plants and new projects. Both investment and luxury spending are subject, inevitably, to more erratic influences and to wider fluctuations than the bread and rent outlays of the $25-week workman. This high-bracket spending and investment was especially susceptible, one may assume, to the crushing news from the stock market in October 1929.

(2) The bad corporate structure. In November 1929, a few weeks after the crash, the Harvard Economic Society gave as a principal reason why a depression need not be feared its reasoned judgement that 'business in most lines has been conducted with prudence and conservatism'.[2] The fact was that American enterprise in the twenties had opened its hospitable arms to an exceptional number of promoters, grafters, swindlers, impostors, and frauds. This, in the long history of such activities, was a kind of flood tide of corporate larceny.

The most important corporate weakness was inherent in the vast new structure of holding companies and investment trusts. The holding companies controlled large segments of the utility, railroad, and entertainment business. Here, as with the investment

1. Selma Goldsmith, George Jaszi, Hyman Kaitz, and Maurice Liebenberg, 'Size Distribution of Income since the Mid-Thirties', *The Review of Economics and Statistics*, February 1954, pp. 16, 18.
2. *Weekly Letter*, 23 November 1929.

trusts, was the constant danger of devastation by reverse leverage. In particular, dividends from the operating companies paid the interest on the bonds of upstream holding companies. The interruption of the dividends meant default on the bonds, bankruptcy, and the collapse of the structure. Under these circumstances, the temptation to curtail investment in operating plant in order to continue dividends was obviously strong. This added to deflationary pressures. The latter, in turn, curtailed earnings and helped bring down the corporate pyramids. When this happened, even more retrenchment was inevitable. Income was earmarked for debt repayment. Borrowing for new investment became impossible. It would be hard to imagine a corporate system better designed to continue and accentuate a deflationary spiral.

(3) The bad banking structure. Since the early thirties, a generation of Americans has been told, sometimes with amusement, sometimes with indignation, often with outrage, of the banking practices of the late twenties. In fact, many of these practices were made ludicrous only by the depression. Loans which would have been perfectly good were made perfectly foolish by the collapse of the borrower's prices or the markets for his goods or the value of the collateral he had posted. The most responsible bankers – those who saw that their debtors were victims of circumstances far beyond their control and sought to help – were often made to look the worst. The bankers yielded, as did others, to the blithe, optimistic, and immoral mood of the times but probably not more so. A depression such as that of 1929–32, were it to begin as this is written, would also be damaging to many currently impeccable banking reputations.

However, although the bankers were not unusually foolish in 1929, the banking structure was inherently weak. The weakness was implicit in the large numbers of independent units. When one bank failed, the assets of others were frozen while depositors elsewhere had a pregnant warning to go and ask for their money. Thus one failure led to other failures, and these spread with a domino effect. Even in the best of times local misfortune or isolated mismanagement could start such a chain reaction. (In the first six months of 1929, 346 banks failed in various parts of the country with aggregate deposits of nearly $115 million.[1]) When income, employment, and values fell as the result of a depression bank failures could quickly become epidemic. This happened after 1929. Again it would be hard to imagine a better arrangement for magnifying the effects of. fear. The weak destroyed not only the other weak, but weakened the strong. People everywhere, rich and poor, were made aware of the disaster by the persuasive intelligence that their savings had been destroyed.

Needless to say, such a banking system, once in the convulsions of failure, had a uniquely repressive effect on the spending of its depositors and the investment of its clients.

(4) The dubious state of the foreign balance. This is a familiar story. During the First World War, the United States became a creditor on international account. In the decade following, the surplus of exports over imports which once had paid the interest and principal on loans from Europe continued. The high tariffs, which restricted imports and helped to create this surplus of exports, remained. However, history and traditional trading habits also accounted for the persistence of the favourable balance, so called.

Before, payments on interest and principal had in effect been deducted from the trade balance. Now that the United States was a creditor, they were added to this balance. The latter, it should be said, was not huge. In only one year (1928) did the excess of exports over imports come to as much as a billion dollars; in 1923 and 1926 it was only about $375,000,000.[2]

1. Compiled from *Federal Reserve Bulletin*, monthly issues, 1929.
2. U.S. Department of Commerce, Bureau of Foreign and Domestic Commerce, *Statistical Abstract of the United States*, 1942.

However, large or small, this difference had to be covered. Other countries which were buying more than they sold, and had debt payments to make in addition, had somehow to find the means for making up the deficit in their transaction with the United States.

During most of the twenties the difference was covered by cash – i.e. gold payments to the United States – and by new private loans by the United States to other countries. Most of the loans were to governments – national, state, or municipal bodies – and a large proportion were to Germany and Central and South America. The underwriters' margins in handling these loans were generous; the public took them up with enthusiasm; competition for the business was keen. If unfortunately corruption and bribery were required as competitive instruments, these were used. In late 1927 Juan Leguia, the son of the President of Peru, was paid $450,000 by J. and W. Seligman and Company and the National City Company (the security affiliate of the National City Bank) for his services in connexion with a $50,000,000 loan which these houses marketed for Peru.[1] Juan's services, according to later testimony, were of a rather negative sort. He was paid for not blocking the deal. The Chase extended President Machado of Cuba, a dictator with a marked predisposition toward murder, a generous personal line of credit which at one time reached $200,000.[2] Machado's son-in-law was employed by the Chase. The bank did a large business in Cuban bonds. In contemplating these loans, there was a tendency to pass quickly over anything that might appear to the disadvantage of the creditor. Mr Victor Schoepperle, a vice-president of the National City Company with the responsibility for Latin American loans, made the following appraisal of Peru as a credit prospect:

Peru: Bad debt record, adverse moral and political risk, bad

1. *Stock Exchange Practices*, Report, 1934, pp. 220–1.
2. ibid., p. 215.

internal debt situation, trade situation about as satisfactory as that of Chile in the past three years. Natural resources more varied. On economic showing Peru should go ahead rapidly in the next ten years.[1]

On such showing the National City Company floated a $15,000,000 loan for Peru, followed a few months later by a $50,000,000 loan, and some ten months thereafter by a $25,000,000 issue. (Peru did prove a highly adverse political risk. President Leguia, who negotiated the loans, was thrown violently out of office, and the loans went into default.)

In all respects these operations were as much a part of the New Era as Shenandoah and Blue Ridge. They were also just as fragile, and once the illusions of the New Era were dissipated they came as abruptly to an end. This, in turn, forced a fundamental revision in the foreign economic position of the United States. Countries could not cover their adverse trade balance with the United States with increased payments of gold, at least not for long. This meant that they had either to increase their exports to the United States or reduce their imports or default on their past loans. President Hoover and the Congress moved promptly to eliminate the first possibility – that the accounts would be balanced by larger imports – by sharply increasing the tariff. Accordingly, debts, including war debts, went into default and there was a precipitate fall in American exports. The reduction was not vast in relation to total output of the American economy, but it contributed to the general distress and was especially hard on farmers.

(5) The poor state of economic intelligence. To regard the people of any time as particularly obtuse seems vaguely improper, and it also establishes a precedent which members of this generation might regret. Yet it seems certain that the economists and those who offered economic counsel in the late

1. *Stock Exchange Practices*, Hearings, February–March 1933, Pt 6, pp. 2091 ff.

twenties and early thirties were almost uniquely perverse. In the months and years following the stock market crash, the burden of reputable economic advice was invariably on the side of measures that would make things worse. In November 1929, Mr Hoover announced a cut in taxes; in the great no-business conferences that followed he asked business firms to keep up their capital investment and to maintain wages. Both of these measures were on the side of increasing spendable income, though unfortunately they were largely without effect. The tax reductions were negligible except in the higher income brackets; businessmen who promised to maintain investment and wages, in accordance with a well-understood convention, considered the promise binding only for the period within which it was not financially disadvantageous to do so. As a result investment outlays and wages were not reduced until circumstances would in any case have brought their reduction.

Still, the effort was in the right direction. Thereafter policy was almost entirely on the side of making things worse. Asked how the government could best advance recovery, the sound and responsible adviser urged that the budget be balanced. Both parties agreed on this. For Republicans the balanced budget was, as ever, high doctrine. But the Democratic Party platform of 1932, with an explicitness which politicians rarely advise, also called for a 'federal budget annually balanced on the basis of accurate executive estimates within revenues ...'

A commitment to a balanced budget is always comprehensive. It then meant there could be no increase in government outlays to expand purchasing power and relieve distress. It meant there could be no further tax reduction. But taken literally it meant much more. From 1930 on the budget was far out of balance, and balance, therefore, meant an increase in taxes, a reduction in spending, or both. The Democratic platform in 1932 called for an 'immediate and drastic reduction of governmental expenditures' to accomplish at least a twenty-five per cent decrease in the cost of government.

The balanced budget was not a subject of thought. Nor was it, as often asserted, a precise matter of faith. Rather it was a formula. For centuries avoidance of borrowing had protected people from slovenly or reckless public housekeeping. Slovenly or reckless keepers of the public purse had often composed complicated arguments to show why balance of income and outlay was not a mark of virtue. Experience had shown that however convenient this belief might seem in the short run, discomfort or disaster followed in the long run. Those simple precepts of a simple world did not hold amid the growing complexities of the early thirties. Mass unemployment in particular had altered the rules. Events had played a very bad trick on people, but almost no one tried to think out the problem anew.

The balanced budget was not the only strait-jacket on policy. There was also the bogy of 'going off' the gold standard and, surprisingly, of risking inflation. Until 1932 the United States added formidably to its gold reserves, and instead of inflation the country was experiencing the most violent deflation in the nation's history. Yet every sober adviser saw dangers here, including the danger of runaway price increases. Americans, though in years now well in the past, had shown a penchant for tinkering with the money supply and enjoying the brief but heady joys of a boom in prices. In 1931 or 1932, the danger or even the feasibility of such a boom was nil. The advisers and counsellors were not, however, analysing the danger or even the possibility. They were serving only as the custodians of bad memories.

The fear of inflation reinforced the demand for the balanced budget. It also limited efforts to make interest rates low, credit plentiful (or at least redundant), and borrowing as easy as possible under the circumstances. Devaluation of the dollar was, of course, flatly ruled out. This directly violated the gold standard rules. At best, in such depression times, monetary policy is a feeble reed on which to lean. The current economic clichés did not allow even the use of that frail weapon. And again, these attitudes were above party. Though himself singularly open-minded, Roosevelt was careful not to offend or disturb his followers. In a speech in Brooklyn toward the close of the 1932 campaign, he said:

> The Democratic platform specifically declares, 'We advocate a sound currency to be preserved at all hazards.' That is plain English. In discussing this platform on 30 July, I said, 'Sound money is an international necessity, not a domestic consideration for one nation alone.' Far up in the Northwest, at Butte, I repeated the pledge . . . In Seattle I reaffirmed my attitude . . .[1]

The following February, Mr Hoover set forth his view, as often before, in a famous letter to the President-elect:

> It would steady the country greatly if there could be prompt assurance that there will be no tampering or inflation of the currency; that the budget will be unquestionably balanced even if further taxation is necessary; that the Government credit will be maintained by refusal to exhaust it in the issue of securities.[2]

The rejection of both fiscal (tax and expenditure) and monetary policy amounted precisely to a rejection of all affirmative government economic policy. The economic advisers of the day had both the unanimity and the authority to force the leaders of both parties to disavow all the available steps to check deflation and depression. In its own way this was a marked achievement – a triumph of dogma over thought. The consequences were profound.

1. Lawrence Sullivan, *Prelude to Panic*, Washington (Statesman Press), 1936, p. 20.
2. William Starr Myers and Walter H. Newton, *The Hoover Administration: A Documented Narrative*, New York (Scribners), 1936, pp. 339–40.

6

It is in light of the above weaknesses of the economy that the role of the stock market crash in the great tragedy of the thirties must be seen. The years of self-depreciation by Wall Street to the contrary, the role is one of respectable importance. The collapse in securities values affected in the first instance the wealthy and the well-to-do. But we see that in the world of 1929 this was a vital group. The members disposed of a large proportion of the consumer income; they were the source of a lion's share of personal saving and investment. Anything that struck at the spending or investment by this group would of necessity have broad effects on expenditure and income in the economy at large. Precisely such a blow was struck by the stock market crash. In addition, the crash promptly removed from the economy the support that it had been deriving from the spending of stock market gains.

The stock market crash was also an exceptionally effective way of exploiting the weaknesses of the corporate structure. Operating companies at the end of the holding-company chain were forced by the crash to retrench. The subsequent collapse of these systems and also of the investment trusts effectively destroyed both the ability to borrow and the willingness to lend for investment. What have long looked like purely fiduciary effects were, in fact, quickly translated into declining orders and increasing unemployment.

The crash was also effective in bringing to an end the foreign lending by which international accounts had been balanced. Now the accounts had, in the main, to be balanced by reduced exports. This put prompt and heavy pressure on export markets for wheat, cotton, and tobacco. Perhaps the foreign loans had only delayed an adjustment in the balance which had one day to come. The stock market crash served nonetheless to precipitate the adjustment with great suddenness at a most unpropitious time. The instinct of farmers who traced their troubles to the stock market was not totally misguided.

Finally, when the misfortune had struck, the attitudes of the time kept anything from being done about it. This, perhaps, was the most disconcerting feature of all. Some people were hungry in 1930 and 1931 and 1932. Others were tortured by the fear that they might go hungry. Yet others suffered the agony of the descent from the honour and respectability that go with income into poverty. And still others feared that they would be next. Meanwhile everyone suffered from a sense of utter hopelessness. Nothing, it seemed, could be done. And given the ideas which controlled policy, nothing could be done.

Had the economy been fundamentally sound in 1929 the effect of the great stock market crash might have been small. Alternatively, the shock to confidence and the loss of spending by those who were caught in the market might soon have worn off. But business in 1929 was not sound; on the contrary it was exceedingly fragile. It was vulnerable to the kind of blow it received from Wall Street. Those who have emphasized this vulnerability are obviously on strong ground. Yet when a greenhouse succumbs to a hailstorm something more than a purely passive role is normally attributed to the storm. One must accord similar significance to the typhoon which blew out of lower Manhattan in October 1929.

7

The military historian when he has finished his chronicle is excused. He is not required to consider the chance for a renewal of war with the Indians, the Mexicans, or the Confederacy. Nor will anyone press him to say how such acrimony can be prevented. But economics is taken more seriously. The economic historian, as a result, is invariably asked whether the misfortunes he describes will afflict us again and how they may be prevented.

The task of this book, as suggested on an early page, is only to tell what happened in 1929. It is not to tell whether or when the misfortunes of 1929 will recur. One of the pregnant lessons of that year will by now be plain: it is that very specific and personal misfortune awaits those who presume to believe that the future is revealed to them. Yet, without undue risk, it may be possible to gain from our view of this useful year some insights into the future. We can distinguish, in particular, between misfortunes that could happen again and others which events, many of them in the aftermath of 1929, have at least made improbable. And we can perhaps see a little of the form and magnitude of the remaining peril.

At first glance the least probable of the misadventures of the late twenties would seem to be another wild boom in the stock market with its inevitable collapse. The memory of that autumn, although now much dimmed, is not yet gone. As those days of disenchantment drew to a close, tens of thousands of Americans shook their heads and muttered, 'Never again'. In every considerable community there are yet a few survivors, aged but still chastened, who are still muttering and still shaking their heads. The New Era had no such guardians of sound pessimism.

Also, there are the new government measures and controls. The powers of the Federal Reserve Board – now styled the Board of Governors, the Federal Reserve System – have been strengthened both in relation to the individual Reserve banks and the member banks. Mitchell's defiance of March 1929 is now unthinkable. What was then an act of arrogant but not abnormal individualism would now be regarded as idiotic. The New York Federal Reserve Bank retains a measure of moral authority and autonomy, but not enough to resist a strong Washington policy. Now also there is power to set margin requirements. If necessary, the speculator can be made to post the full price of the stock he buys. While this may not completely discourage him, it does mean that when the market falls there can be no outsurge of margin calls to force further sales and insure that the liquidation will go through continuing spasms. Finally, the Securities and Exchange Commission is, one hopes, effective to large-scale market manipulation, and it also keeps rein on the devices and the salesmanship by which new speculators are recruited.

Yet, in some respects, the chances for a recurrence of a speculative orgy are rather good. No one can doubt that the American people remain susceptible to the speculative mood – to the conviction that enterprise can be attended by unlimited rewards in which they, individually, were meant to share. A rising market can still bring the reality of riches. This, in turn, can draw more and more people to participate. The government preventatives and controls are ready. In the hands of a determined government their efficacy cannot be doubted. There are, however, a hundred reasons why a government will determine not to use them. In our democracy an election is in the offing even on the day after an election. The avoidance of depression and prevention of unemployment have become for the politician the most critical of all questions of public policy. Action to break up a boom must always be weighed against the chance that it will cause unemployment at a politically inopportune moment. Booms, it must be noted, are not stopped until after they have started. And after they have started the action will always look, as it did to the frightened men in the Federal Reserve Board in February 1929, like a decision in favour of immediate as against ultimate death. As we have seen, the immediate death not only had the disadvantage of being immediate but of identifying the executioner.

The market will not go on a speculative rampage without some rationalization. But during the next boom some newly rediscovered virtuosity of the free enterprise system will be cited. It will be pointed out that people are justified in paying the present prices – indeed, almost any price – to have an equity position in the system. Among the first to accept these rationalizations will be some of those responsible for invoking the controls. They will say firmly that controls are not needed. The newspapers, some of them, will agree and speak harshly of those who think action might be in order. They will be called men of little faith.[1]

## 8

A new adventure in stock market speculation sometime in the future followed by another collapse would not have the same effect on the economy as in 1929. Whether it would show the economy to be fundamentally sound or unsound is something, unfortunately, that will not be wholly evident until after the event. There can be no question, however, that many of the points of extreme weakness exposed in 1929 or soon thereafter have since been substantially strengthened. The distribution of income is no longer quite so lopsided. Between 1929 and 1948 the share of total personal income going to the five per cent of the population with the highest income dropped from nearly a third to less than a fifth of the total. Between 1929 and 1950 the share of all family income which was received as wages, salaries, pensions, and unemployment compensation increased from approximately sixty-one per cent to approximately seventy-one per cent. This is the income of everyday people. Although dividends, interest, and rent, the income characteristically of the well-to-do, increased in total amount, the share dropped from just over twenty-two to just over twelve per cent of total family personal income.[2]

1. In warning in 1960 of the current speculation, I managed to attract, in a modest way, this epithet.

2. These data are from Goldsmith et al., 'Size of Distribution of Income', pp. 16, 18.

Similarly, in the years since 1929, the great investment trust promotions have been folded up and put away, or they have become cautious and respectable. The S.E.C., aided by the bankruptcy laws, has flattened out the great utility holding company pyramids. Federal insurance of bank deposits, even to this day, has not been given full credit for the revolution that it has worked in the nation's banking structure. With this one piece of legislation the fear which operated so efficiently to transmit weakness was dissolved. As a result the grievous defect of the old system by which failure begot failure, was cured. Rarely has so much been accomplished by a single law.

The problem of the foreign balance is much changed from what it was twenty-five years ago. Now the United States finds itself with the propensity to buy or spend as much and more than it sells and receives. And now any disequilibrium is filled or more than filled by military aid, Export-Import and International Bank loans and economic aid. In contrast with the loans to Latin American republics and the German municipalities, these payments are relatively invulnerable to shock. A crash in the stock market would affect them but little if at all.

Finally, there has been a modest accretion of economic knowledge. A developing depression would not now be met with a fixed determination to make it worse. Without question no-business conferences would be assembled at the White House. We would see an explosion of reassurance and incantation. Many would urge waiting and hoping as the best policy. Not again, however, would people suppose that the best policy would be – as Secretary Mellon so infelicitously phrased it – to 'liquidate labour, liquidate stocks, liquidate the farmers, liquidate real estate'.[1] Our determination to deal firmly and adequately with a serious depression is still to be tested. But there is still a considerable difference between a failure to do

1. Quoted by Herbert Hoover, *Memoirs*, p. 30.

enough that is right and a determination to do much that is wrong.

Other weaknesses in the economy have been corrected. The much maligned farm programme provides a measure of security for farm income and therewith for spending by farmers. Unemployment compensation accomplishes the same result, if still inadequately, for labour. The remainder of the social security system – pensions and public assistance – helps protect the income and consequently the expenditure of yet other segments of the population. The tax system is a far better servant of stability than it was in 1929. An angry god may have endowed capitalism with inherent contradictions. But at least as an afterthought he was kind enough to make social reform surprisingly consistent with improved operation of the system.

### 9

Yet all this reinforcement notwithstanding, it would probably be unwise to expose the economy to the shock of another major speculative collapse. Some of the new reinforcements might buckle. Instead of the investment trusts we have the mutual funds and the contraction here would be sharp. Fissures might open at other new and perhaps unexpected places. Even the quick withdrawal from the economy of the spending that comes from stock market gains might be damaging. Any collapse, even though the further consequences were small, would not be good for the public reputation of Wall Street.

Wall Street, in recent times, has become, as a learned phrase has it, very 'public relations conscious'. Since a speculative collapse can only follow a speculative boom, one might expect that Wall Street would lay a heavy hand on any resurgence of speculation. The Federal Reserve would be asked by bankers and brokers to lift margins to the limit; it would be warned to enforce the requirement sternly against those who might try to borrow on their own stocks and bonds in order to buy more of them. The public would be warned sharply and often of the risks inherent in buying stocks for the rise. Those who persisted, nonetheless, would have no one to blame but themselves. The position of the Stock Exchange, its members, the banks, and the financial community in general would be perfectly clear and as well protected in the event of a further collapse as sound public relations allow.

As noted, all this might logically be expected. It will not come to pass. This is not because the instinct for self-preservation in Wall Street is poorly developed. On the contrary, it is probably normal and may be above. But now, as throughout history, financial capacity and political perspicacity are inversely correlated. Long-run salvation by men of business has never been highly regarded if it means disturbance of orderly life and convenience in the present. So inaction will be advocated in the present even though it means deep trouble in the future. Here, at least equally with communism, lies the threat to capitalism. It is what causes men who know that things are going quite wrong to say that things are fundamentally sound.

# INDEX

Acceptances, 57, 67

Agriculture, 31; farm programme, 209; and stock market, 203–4; weakness of economy, 199–200. *See also* Farmers

Aktiebolaget Kreuger and Toll. *See* Kreuger and Toll

Aldrich, Winthrop W., 168–9

*All Quiet on the Western Front*, 107

Alleghany Corporation, 41, 76

Allen, Frederick Lewis, 34–5*n*., 40*n*., 98*n*., 101, 106, 123, 133*n*., 137*n*., 162*n*.

Allied Chemical and Dye, 88

American Can, 134, 140

American Company, 88

American Founders Group, 80, 84–5, 161

American Insuranstocks Corporation, 89

*The American Magazine*, 95

American Railway Express, 62

American Stores, 71

American Telephone and Telegraph Company, 88, 99, 107–8, 120, 131, 144, 161

American Tobacco, 70

American Trust Company, 88

Anaconda Copper, 161

Anglo-American Shares, Inc., 89

Angly, Edward, 109*n*., 162*n*.

Aquinas, Saint Thomas, 99

Armour and Company, 166

Arndt, H. W., 192*n*., 193*n*.

Associated Gas and Electric, **71**, 128

Astor, Vincent, 151

*The Atlantic Monthly*, 81

Auburn Automobile, 146

Axley, Seth, 65

Ayres, Colonel Leonard P., **127**

Babe Ruth, 107

Babson, Roger W., 118, 120, **146**; Annual National Business Conference, 108–9; Babson break, 108–10; election forecast, 43–4

Bagehot, Walter, 59, 72*n*., 155, 188

Baker, George F., Jr, 123*n*.

Balance of payments. *See* Foreign balance

Balanced budget, a formula, 200–1; Whitney and, 175–6

Baldwin Locomotive Works, 128

Bank of England, 38, 60

Bank of France, 38

Bankers, bear raid denied, 135–7; loss of prestige, 165–6, 177–8; optimism of, 96; Pecora committee, 174; speculation of officers in their own stocks, 168, 169–70; support ended, 132–3, 135; support market, 122–6, 127–8

Bankers Trust Company, 123

Banks, failures, 196–7; federal insurance of deposits, 208; in another crisis, 210; out-of-town banks recall money

211

# FOR THE BEST IN PAPERBACKS, LOOK FOR THE 🐧

In every corner of the world, on every subject under the sun, Penguin represents quality and variety – the very best in publishing today.

For complete information about books available from Penguin – including Pelicans, Puffins, Peregrines and Penguin Classics – and how to order them, write to us at the appropriate address below. Please note that for copyright reasons the selection of books varies from country to country.

---

**In the United Kingdom:** For a complete list of books available from Penguin in the U.K., please write to *Dept E.P., Penguin Books Ltd, Harmondsworth, Middlesex, UB7 0DA*

**In the United States:** For a complete list of books available from Penguin in the U.S., please write to *Dept BA, Penguin, 299 Murray Hill Parkway, East Rutherford, New Jersey 07073*

**In Canada:** For a complete list of books available from Penguin in Canada, please write to *Penguin Books Canada Ltd, 2801 John Street, Markham, Ontario L3R 1B4*

**In Australia:** For a complete list of books available from Penguin in Australia, please write to the *Marketing Department, Penguin Books Australia Ltd, P.O. Box 257, Ringwood, Victoria 3134*

**In New Zealand:** For a complete list of books available from Penguin in New Zealand, please write to the *Marketing Department, Penguin Books (NZ) Ltd, Private Bag, Takapuna, Auckland 9*

**In India:** For a complete list of books available from Penguin, please write to *Penguin Overseas Ltd, 706 Eros Apartments, 56 Nehru Place, New Delhi, 110019*

**In Holland:** For a complete list of books available from Penguin in Holland, please write to *Penguin Books Nederland B.V., Postbus 195, NL–1380AD Weesp, Netherlands*

**In Germany:** For a complete list of books available from Penguin, please write to *Penguin Books Ltd, Friedrichstrasse 10 – 12, D–6000 Frankfurt Main 1, Federal Republic of Germany*

**In Spain:** For a complete list of books available from Penguin in Spain, please write to *Longman Penguin España, Calle San Nicolas 15, E–28013 Madrid, Spain*